NORWAY
behind the Scenery

ARVID BRYNE
JOAN HENRIKSEN

NORWAY
behind the Scenery

J.W. CAPPELENS FORLAG A·S

CONTENT

FOREWORD

We come from backgrounds that are just about as different as possible: Joan was born in Philadelphia and grew up in the Midwestern USA, Arvid was born and brought up in Stavanger on Norway's west coast. Circumstances, and some sort of predictable fate, led to our both becoming journalists. Before we met, Joan had moved to Norway and Stavanger; Arvid had moved to Oslo and New York and back to Oslo.

When we met each other for the first time, on jobs for our respective newspapers, we talked about bread. Then we chatted about potatoes. Eventually we realized we were talking about Stavanger and Norway and Norwegians. Since then the conversations have continued.

Why are Norwegian towns empty at Easter? Why do all Norwegians head for snow and freezing temperatures in the mountains each Spring as the sun finally begins to shine? Do Norwegians have a love life? How did it happen that a people who were so poor became so rich?

The questions bubbled up. Here and there answers, or an explanation, surfaced. Since we work at opposite ends of the country, our dialogue eventually took on written form. Naturally we both realized all the time that we weren't writing just for fun: We don't use our precious free time to write, without the result becoming a manuscript.

What Joan wrote first was a title: "Norway Behind the Scenery." Not to be bested, Arvid chose a title from an old drinking song from the 1700's: "For Norge, Kjempers Fødeland" (birthplace of the giants). Joan's was possible to translate but no foreigner would understand the irony in Arvid's.

This was the only problem we had with this book. Otherwise the work has been play and pleasure.

Oslo/Stavanger, Spring 1986

Joan Felicia Henriksen   Arvid Bryne

NORWAY – BIRTHPLACE OF THE GIANTS?

ARVID: "By the way, what's it like in Norway?" New York's Mayor, Ed Koch, suddenly interrupted his stream of words to ask me the question. The interviewer and the subject had changed roles.

"Norway is the most beautiful country in the world. Altogether the nation has fewer people than go to work on an ordinary day in Manhattan. Almost all are the same race. They talk the same language. They are members of the same church, but almost no one goes to church. They go to the same schools, eat the same food, read the same newspapers, choose between programs shown on one television channel and are born with skis on . . ."

Before I could draw a breath to continue, he threw up his hands and exclaimed:

"My God it must be boring!"

* * *

Norwegians, of course, don't share his opinion. They're convinced that they're among the luckiest people on the globe. They don't spend most of each Sunday pouring through all the sections of the Sunday paper before going out to a late lunch. Sunday papers are illegal; and when people in Europe and the USA are going out to friendly restaurants, the Norwegian is sitting alone on a mountain top munching on a homemade sandwich from a lunch bag.

Sure Norway is in Europe, but so close to its farthest reaches that we have so far scornfully managed to avoid all attempts to get us to become a part of an integrated European fellowship. We are enough unto ourselves, as Henrik Ibsen put it in "Peer Gynt."

When Norwegians enter a train compartment, the first person to arrive goes to one corner. The next one seats himself as far away as possible, diagonally in the opposite corner. The third and the fourth person each take the remaining corners, and only after these places are full, will the middle fill up. Those who take the middle will have first searched through the entire train to try to find compartments with better seats. Everyone who has traveled by train in Southern Europe knows that the opposite occurs there. Southern Europeans avoid loneliness, we seek it.

JOAN: Norway and the Norwegians are unique. But it can take a while to see all the differences. At first meeting the new resident non-Norwegian tends to see only the similarities: clothing, jobs, most habits, religion, housing, general appearance. But first impressions are deceptive. It is only after living here a while, and beginning to master the shades of meaning in the language, that the subtle but very present individual differences make themselves felt.

It is certain that sooner or later every foreigner living in Norway will hear this question from the Norwegians: "Don't you find the Norwegians

. . . when people in Europe and the USA are going out to friendly restaurants, the Norwegian is sitting alone on a mountain top munching on a homemade sandwich from a lunch bag.

too cold? Or reserved? Aren't they hard to get to know? Or unfriendly?" Wherever I've been in Norway, without exception, this question has come up eventually.

Equally certain is that this question will make me uncomfortable. First, because it invites a negative answer and I am a guest in this country. Second, because I've never really believed it was true that Norwegians were too cold, too reserved, too hard to get to know, or unfriendly.

What is absolutely true is that the Norwegians are convinced it is a fact. They put themselves down, and say they regret it – and also admit they wouldn't know how to change. They admit, as Arvid says, that they seek out isolation, invite loneliness.

This amateur observer of the Norwegian way of life, and student of Norwegian history, has evolved the theory that Norwegian "reserve" is a survival characteristic that has come about over centuries of living with isolation in a hundred lonely valleys or on the sides of mountains. Reserve, inner resources, a genuine sense of self-being-enough has been needed when battling the harsh and unfriendly forces of nature.

ARVID: Although some of our Norwegian cities have histories

△Norwegians have the reputation, worldwide, of being hard-working, diligent, healthy, honest and straight-forward.

Isolated homes perch like sentinels on the side of ▽ the mountain.

stretching back a thousand years, and even though most Norwegians today live in well-populated areas, we have never become city dwellers. Everytime we have a day or two off – which is quite often – we go to a cottage in the mountains, the forest or at the seaside. Most Norwegians believe that for a vacation spot to be ideal there must be no neighbors for miles around.

JOAN: Drive along any fjord and look at the lonely, isolated homes perched like sentinels on the side of the mountain. I was drawn to them first while driving along Sørfjorden, an arm of the Hardangerfjord, between Odda and Kinsarvik. I was on highway 47 looking across the fjord at pocket farms sitting precariously on what appeared to be narrow ledges, many hundreds of meters up from the water's edge. On my side, the road side, their car might be parked.

Driving on past Kinsarvik on highway 7, alongside Eidfjorden, we saw many isolated homes - white and neat - clinging tenaciously to the side of the mountain above the water.

Summer pasturing on the old mountain farms is still practiced in some places.

I was told these people would travel by rowboat to the nearest settlement or store for the staples they could not produce themselves. I was told stories of how they struggled through winters, enduring childbirth, illness, hunger, in the days before telephones, motors for boats, or the automobile parked across the fjord. When the story tellers saw my amazement they assured me that those on the mountainside farms liked their life, thrived on being a part of nature, blossomed there like the trees which were planted to hold the soil.

Being independent, self-reliant, and careful not to be overwhelmed by emotions, became survival characteristics for Norwegians. People who did not have these characteristics would probably leave the isolated areas for towns. At the very least they would not be the first choice of a man or woman looking for a suitable spouse. Strong and silent would choose strong and silent, and raise strong and silent children.

This isolation explains another peculiarly Norwegian tradition: parties that go on all night and periodic drunkenness. Imagine the Hardanger wedding made famous in song and paintings. The guests traveled sometimes for days to arrive at the wedding party. It was a

Pheasants were imported to Norway as late as 1870.

welcome, yes, sanity-saving break in the long and endless work cycle. It was a time to eat too much, drink too much, dance until you dropped. It might be a year or two before there would be another party, another chance to catch up on all the news and gossip.

Modern Norwegians only rarely give a party, but when they do it is elaborate and can last until the wee hours. Informal "drop-in" get-

It's no wonder almost every Norwegian is a poet.

togethers are rare: it's an invasion of privacy. The regular party, then, because it is so seldom, seems never to end – almost like the wedding party that lasted for days. The long Norwegian party can come as quite a surprise to the uninformed newcomer.

The Norwegians have the reputation, worldwide, of being hard-working, diligent, healthy, honest and straight-forward. It's a reputation the Norwegians want very much to believe in and live by. They also accept with resignation that these sterling qualities lead others to think them often stolid, dull, unimaginative. Since the first outweighs the second the Norwegian resigns himself to the fact that others often find him stodgy.

Unfortunately, as the 21st century approaches, they see their way of life being eroded, their youth showing the same restlessness and dissatisfaction that is disturbing other nations. The crime rate has doubled and is endlessly debated, even though it is still the lowest in the Nordic lands.

Norwegians want very much to live in a welfare state, with the sick, the weak and the old provided for. Yet they do not really want to sacrifice individual free enter-prise, especially now that times are good.

ARVID: Today industrial developments, not to mention the rich oil and gas finds in the North Sea, have radically changed the Norwegian lifestyle and living standard. We are no longer among the poorest in

▽ The Condeeps grow slowly, in Gandsfjord, Stavanger. Norwegian Contractors provided the town with a new nighttime silhouette, one we watched and grew used to, and missed when the oil rig was towed out to sea.

◁ Mining at Svalbard in the old days.

Agriculture has also been modernised. ▷

Europe; we are one of the richest nations in the world.

Only to a small extent has the new wealth changed us. We still complain over gas prices and income tax – with good reason, according to many – and we are still singing the old song: For Norge, kjempers fødeland, (birthplace of the giants) with great seriousness.

And when the long, cold winter begins to draw to a close, when the first flowers begin to show themselves and the sun begins to warm the earth, we load up our backpack and take to the mountains at Easter.

To battle the snow and the elements one more time? No, to feel the sun up close, to celebrate that once more the light has defeated the winter dark, to glide down over smooth mountainsides and warm ourselves in front of an open fire-place in the evening. To use our country and acknowledge that the magnificent scenery is a greater resource than the black gold at the bottom of the North Sea.

JOAN: This struggle to tame and soften progress, to hold on to all the old traditions – to perhaps "have their cake and eat it too," is shaping modern Norway as surely as the hard times of the past pushed second and third sons to leave and settle elsewhere.

Norway has been called "the national park of Europe." Its spectacular beauty is overwhelmingly awe-inspiring. But this same loveliness is also back-breakingly difficult. Norway's people have been tempered by the deceptive nature of the beauty, the truth behind the scenery.

Welcome to the real Norway, the Norway camouflaged by the impressive scenery. This Norway, the Norway of fascinating and different people, of industrial growth, of new riches, awaits your exploration.

A MODERN NATION

JOAN: Once upon a time Viking long ships claimed Norwegian territorial waters as their own.

Once upon a time much later, graceful white sails danced quietly and smoothly against the sky.

Once upon a time there came billowing black clouds of smoke issuing from steamships plying these northern seas.

Tucked in between Viking ships at anchor, sailing ships on a visit, steamships unloading cargo, there were always and ever the small proud fishing vessels. One, two, perhaps more craggy-faced fishermen would look up from their endless work with nets and lines and wonder if life might be better aboard the larger ships, without the ever-present smell of fish.

Today's North Sea has a different silhouette against the horizon. Strange awkward looking oil platforms, without a single sleek sailing line, are towed from fjord to the deep ocean – to become entire cities at sea. Monster crane ships fill harbors that once overflowed with herring. Ever more gigantic cruise ships sail up countless fjords bringing tourists from as far away as China who are curious about this country: Norway. Norway – whose name meant Land of the North or the North Way to the world one thousand years ago. Norway, whose name means that today.

And still, bobbing between the platforms, avoiding the wake of the cruise ship, can be seen the small wooden fishing boats, looking even more vulnerable today than they did a few hundred years ago.

What is Norway?

JOAN: Is today's Norway modern? Is Norway up-to-date? Or is it living with one foot in the distant, romanticized past and one in the dreamer's 21st century?

The visitor to the fjords or the small villages anywhere in this country exclaims over the thatched roofs, the wooden houses built as they were built 150 years ago, the fish set out to dry in the air as they have been for as long as man has fished the coastal waters.

Behind the tourist's Norway there is another country: a country making advanced electronic equipment; a nation reclaiming oil and gas from ever deeper and more treacherous waters, using ever more advanced techniques; a nation striving to become an international economic force through the sale of products and expertise.

One fact is incontrovertible: Norway in the second half of the 1980's is successful. It is rich and getting richer.

From need to riches

ARVID: Over a period covering just about a hundred years, Norway has gone from being a poor and underdeveloped land to one of the

The new and the old silhouette in the North Sea – the graceful sailing lady is dwarfed by the gigantic oil rig.

△ In 1868 one-fifth of the residents of Christiania (Oslo), lived in poverty. Infant mortality was 30 percent.

◁ Today's Norwegian has the highest living standard in the world – and the most leisure time to enjoy it.

richest in the world. Today the gross national product of Norway is 60 times what it was in 1830. During the same period the population has quadrupled.

This means that each Norwegian now produces fifteen times more than his forefathers did 150 years ago. At that time a large part of the population lived at, or near, the poverty level.

Descendents of the Norwegians who emigrated then and afterwards, shake their heads over the fact that their ancestors left this country, where today the living is so good. These people ought to take a trip to the Folk Museum in Oslo. Despite the fact that the old homes there look romantic, with their small windows and the grass on the roof, they felt less so when there was sour smoke trapped under the roof, cold and drafty walls, runny-nosed children of all ages, clothes that had to be dried, and food that had to be prepared – usually all in the same room. These houses which have been preserved are only samples of how the poor lived.

Good old days? My father, who was born in Stavanger in 1885, had very little comprehension of the expression "the good old days." My grandfather was a blacksmith and worked at Stavanger Foundry and Dry-dock. My father was one of a family of nine who lived in two small rooms plus a kitchen which they shared with another family. In order to help finances at home my father quit school when he was 12 years old and began to work as an errand boy and helper to a butcher. Like so many others he didn't see any future in Stavanger. When he was 16 he emigrated to the USA. The first year he was a farmhand in North Dakota and later he moved to Chicago and worked in the stockyards, in the slaughterhouse. My father, however, began to be overwhelmed by homesickness, and after five years in "God's Own Country," he boarded a boat to re-cross the Atlantic.

When he died in 1963, he was aware that Poor-Norway had become Welfare-Norway. But he never completely believed that what had happened was real. My father was one of 900,000 Norwegians who, between 1865 and 1930, left for the USA, Canada, South America and Australia. Most of them went to the USA. Compared to the population (about two million in 1890), only Ireland had a greater emigration. Today there are about four million Americans of Norwegian descent – just as many Norwegians as there are in Norway. My father was not, of course, the only one who came home to the old country. When the great emigration wave ended in 1930 it was calculated that approximately one in four of the emigrants had returned home.

JOAN: My husband, who left Norway when he was 15 years old and finally became an American citizen, managed to get a work permit in Norway in 1977, two years after the immigration stop had been put into effect. Einar came in under an unwritten "Prodigal Son" clause. As the Alien Office official said: "Anybody who was born in Norway, who has any sense, will of course come home."

Warm clothes, a hole drilled in the ice, and a nearby lake becomes a source of winter food.

△ Primary production employed the majority of workers in earlier times.

There are still many tiny farms where old-fashioned methods are in use. Perhaps he likes it this way, more likely the farm is too small to justify major purchases of heavy equipment.   ▷

▽ The Sunday farmer – pictured as the national romantics saw them, in clean clothes.

Better life

ARVID: At the close of the last century about 70 percent of the labor force was engaged in agriculture, forestry and fishing. Today it is eight percent. A worker in 1870 had to labor one day (and what a day – 12 to 14 hours was usual) in order to buy 10 kilos of flour. Today a person works 20 minutes in order to be able to afford the same flour. He had to work half a day to buy 10 kilos of potatoes, and one and three-quarter days to buy a kilo of butter. Today a person earns enough in 15 minutes to buy both.

Clothes are much cheaper and easier to get. Cotton goods were, in the last century, a luxury only the rich could afford. Most people wore wool. It's no secret that the road from grass via sheep to wool and then finished clothes is both long and arduous. The industrial revolution brought inexpensive cotton goods and a revolution in clothing possibilities. No less impressive have been the improvements in other areas of life, with the raising of the housing standards and the expansion of public services – in particular health and education.

Before 1830 the greater part of the population was illiterate. Doctors and hospital services were almost nonexistent and were, when they were to be found, only for the rich. It is not, primarily, the expansion of the modern health system which has made it possible for people today to live so much longer and to be so much healthier than they were 100 years ago.

Diet plays a large role. In those days porridge, potatoes, and salt fish were the staple items for most people – although people on the coast also ate fresh fish. Since then meat, fruit and vegetables have come to be daily fare. Life expectancy at birth has gone from age 48 in 1830 to age 78 today for women; from 45 to 72 for men. What is even more noticeable is that deaths at all ages have decreased greatly.

The biggest drop is for newborns. In the 1830's there were 13 babies dying for every 100 born, in the first year of life. Today one baby in every thousand dies.

"I didn't know any good old days," my father said.

The dream chasers

JOAN: In 1879 my great-grandfather, Samuel Ingebretsen, sold his farm in Trøndelag, sold all his possessions, and taking his wife and two children left Norway for the land of opportunity – America.

In 1977, almost 100 years later, I, his great-granddaughter, sold my home and all my possessions in Midwestern America, and with my husband left America for the "land of promise" – Norway.

Today Norway appears to be the land of opportunity thanks to North Sea oil and gas and an incredible wave of good fortune over the past 20 years. But the country is much too small, with too little arable land, to welcome immigrants indiscriminately.

Nevertheless Norway accepts quite a good number of refugees each year, from Iran, Bangladesh, Asia and Africa. Those accepted are provided with homes, education and help from professionals to adapt to this environment.

Norwegians would like to think they are free of prejudice, but there remains a large group that would prefer keeping Norway for the Norwegians. A recent survey showed that 50 percent of all Norwegians would rather not have foreigners living in Norway – no matter where the foreigner comes from. But the survey also showed it was those people who had the least contact with foreigners who still had the most prejudices. Among those who deal with foreigners living in Norway there was less prejudice. That's a healthy sign.

In 1983 Sagene School in Oslo was the object of threats – the foreign students were not to march in the May 17th parade. The result was worth the threats – the Norwegian children surrounded the darker skinned newcomers protectively and half the Storting marched with the children.

Many immigrants to Norway have taken jobs Norwegians no longer want – and the fact that they are willing to work longer hours, seven days a week, creates other conflicts.

The culture conflicts are obvious as the photo shows – learning the language is one key solution

There is a sense of being my brother's keeper. Therefore it is official policy that when a foreigner does come here he/she should have the same opportunities as a Norwegian. Norway is an egalitarian society and wishes no outcasts, perhaps for its own good as much as for the foreigner's. This means that foreigners get free courses in Norwegian and the children receive classes in their mother tongue so they won't suffer.

But very few Norwegians welcome these strangers with different color skin to the extent of opening their homes to them.

As Norway entered what could be called its current "Golden Age," in 1975, just as the oil was really beginning to make the nation rich, an immigration stop was put into effect. This means that a foreigner (as against the official refugee or person seeking political asylum) has to have a specific skill or profession needed by Norwegian society, in order to be granted a work and residence permit.

Growth

ARVID: The greatest gift which nature has given to Norwegians is not the North Sea oil, the fjords, the mountains or other resources. It is the

Gulf Stream. Because of it we have temperatures we can live with both summer and winter. The mild ocean stream which comes to us across the Atlantic from the Gulf of Mexico means that we have ice-free seas all year round and winter temperatures that are comparable with those much further south.

This is truly unusual because Oslo lies on the same latitude as parts of Greenland and Alaska. Norway's, and the world's northernmost city, Hammerfest, lies on a parallel with the glaciers of Greenland and Point Barrow, Alaska's northernmost point.

Mountainous problems

JOAN: Geographical conditions aggravate problems. Companies located in remote areas struggle with high transportation costs and many other disadvantages.

△ The rescue service follows the Norwegian to the mountains. Thousands of volunteers, and trained dogs, are available to search the wilderness areas for skiers lost or injured.

E 76 over Haukeli. ▷

Although the shortest distance north–south is but 1,752 kilometers, these figures begin to swell when the coastline is added. Just the coastline, without fjords and bays counted, measures 2,650 kilometers. Now add the fjords and bays and the length of Norway's coast becomes 21,347 kilometers. To go from here to there by highway in Norway often also means many slow ferry trips following a long wait for the ferry to arrive. There are still towns in Northern Norway without rail

connection with the rest of Norway. And then there are the 50,000 islands along the coast, many of which are inhabited. Vast distances. Often extremely poor communication.

A former Ambassador from the United States to Norway said publicly that this country was really two nations. "Even the weather map is divided in two," he said, pointing to the television set. He'd be even more sarcastic today since Svalbard (Spitzbergen) has been connected to the television sending system. There is now a small box in the left hand corner of the TV screen showing the small island – still another part of this extended nation. Until very recently there were thousands of homes in this country without telephones. The waiting time for a phone could be two or three years, sometimes longer if the area was remote. There are still many areas without TV reception simply because the small population does not warrant the work and expense necessary to build the relay stations.

Shipping

ARVID: "Our honor and our power have been given us by the white sails," wrote Norwegian author Bjørnstjerne Bjørnson as early as 1868. He was right. Shipping and trading in lumber have, more than anything else, laid the foundation for Norwegian economic growth. Just in the period from 1850 to 1875 the numbers of Norwegian seamen rose from 15,000 to 60,000, and the size of the fleet was increased fivefold. In this period Norway passed Spain, Holland, Germany and France as a shipping power, and reached third place worldwide.

How could this happen in a country where so little capital was to be found? In most countries, except Norway, the fleet was concentrated in a few large cities, with large shipowners and a wealthy environment. Here the problem was solved by forming "part owners," a form of ownership which compares with today's stockholding companies. But instead of buying shares the Norwegians of that time became part-owners in a ship by helping to build it, by delivering lumber, or otherwise sharing in the process. In this way a ship could be jointly owned by an entire small town or village, and on the southern coast it was usual to combine being a farmer and a shipowner. This form of ownership structure worked very well in the days of the sailing ships, but it became a hindrance when the transition to steamships began, particularly because it tried to ignore the competition from ships built of iron (most often in other countries).

Norway was particularly late when it came to making the change from sails to steam, a fact which was unfortunate. Because of this, when the next change came, from steam to motor, we were quicker off the mark than any other nation. The First World War was a critical and decisive period for Norwegian shipping. Since Norway was neutral the Norwegian shipowners had many opportunities and made a great deal of money. At the same time the war, and particularly the unrestricted submarine warfare, resulted in large losses of ships and men.

Between the wars the fleet was modernized and expanded, and when the Second World War broke out we had the most modern fleet in the world. It was also the fourth largest after Great Britain, the USA and Japan. After the war started the merchant fleet was put at the disposal of the Norwegian government in exile in London, which, in this way, provided a fleet of more than 1,000 ships. These came to play an exceptionally important role for the combined allied forces. Approximately one third of all the oil which was shipped from the USA to Great Britain was on Norwegian ships. The percentage for other goods was even greater.

During the allied invasion Norwegian ships and men also played an important role. Over the five war years, 3,392 Norwegian seamen died, and about half the tonnage was lost.

Money from air

ARVID. A well-known and popular theme in Norwegian folk tales is about the boy who kills a troll and finds a huge treasure of gold and

An industrial development center, such as Norsk Hydro's on Herøya, outside Porsgrunn, is rare. Skien can be seen in the background. This was originally Hydro's primary storage and shipping center for fertilizer products manufactured in Rjukan and Notodden.

silver in the troll's home in the mountain. Even more unbelievable is the true tale of a Norwegian industry making great amounts of money out of air.

Norsk Hydro was established in 1905 by Sam Eyde who, with Kristian Birkeland, developed the electric arc furnace. By using this they were able to produce nitric acid from the air's nitrogen. The nitric acid was then used to make nitrates, which are the main ingredient in artificial fertilizer.

Norsk Hydro was started with Swedish, French and some Norwegian capital. The reason why it was good business for foreign capital to invest in such a project in Norway was, of course, Norway's cheap water power. The development of the waterfalls had begun slowly, in the last 15 years before the turn of the century, and Norsk Hydro had been a pioneer here, too. They built new towns, halfway up on a mountain in, for instance, Rjukan in Telemark; because that was the home of the mighty Rjukan waterfall which was tamed and sent through pipelines.

By the end of the 1960's Norsk Hydro needed more than seven billion kilowatts of electricity a year. This was equal to 13 percent of the electricity consumption for the whole of Norway in 1968.

An industrial Cinderella

JOAN: In fact Norsk Hydro did a brilliant job of harnessing the Rjukan waterfall by lifting it 100 meters further up the mountain and letting it run a short way through steel pipelines to make electricity. And still it pours through its natural pathway occasionally, to impress visitors.

Norsk Hydro then created two new urban communities in a wilderness area of Telemark and provided lifesaving work for the area. Production at Notodden and Rjukan made Norway the first nation that could export fertilizer made from air and water. On the technical side the installations were revolutionary and the huge generating stations and factories maintained for many years the aura of immensity and mystery. Norsk Hydro, like the nation, weathered good times and bad, changing industrialization, depressions and wars to sell to the world fertilizer market.

Then oil came along in the 50's to push coal out of the market as the dominant raw material in the chemical industry. More changes were needed. It was only natural, if not imperative, that Norsk Hydro should be looking for oil, along with the French, as early as 1963. Hydro had a modest 6.7 percent share of Ekofisk and then became a partner in the Frigg gas field discovered in 1971.

ARVID: Today the need for electricity is not the same, because Norsk Hydro makes its products based on oil. This has led to the growth of a large petro-chemical industry and production of a large list of products. Artificial fertilizer is still being made, but out of the same raw material is now coming the plastic packaging it is shipped in, hartshorn salt for baking, dry ice, neon, magnesium, plastic raw material for polyvinylchloride (PVC), aluminum and much more.

Norsk Hydro was also the Norwegian company (about 68 percent of the shares are Norwegian owned) which invested most in the development of oil and gas in the North Sea as early as the 1970's.

JOAN: In December, 1985, Norsk Hydro was 80 years old and it had invested 20 billion kroner in Norway and abroad over the past five years, without increasing its debt load. Its turnover in 1985 was 40 billion kroner, making it one of Scandinavia's largest companies. And the Cinderella company also controlled the largest of the new and upcoming industries in Norway – the fish farming company of Mowi.

Work for all

JOAN: As late as 1950 Norway could be said to be poor. The nation was struggling to recover from the effects of the long German occupation during World War II that had come when the country was already beaten down by the depression of the 1930's. The fishing industry had never been able to make all the necessary adjustments after the herring began to disappear. Norway's merchant fleet, which once dominated the sea, was struggling to recover from the long war.

ARVID: The major motto for the politics of reconstruction after WWII in Norway was "work for everybody." While there had been disagreement on this subject before the war, the mutual experiences during the war meant there was an entirely new attitude toward equalization, rapprochement and equality of status. Reconstruction following WWII is said to have taken five years.

The direct aid from the USA via the Marshall Plan helped considerably. Norway received 2,500 million kroner. This was equal to one-tenth of all Norway's net investments in the first ten years following the war. Capital investments led to a strong and even growth for Norwegian industry and shipping which didn't break down until the international oil crisis in the beginning of the 1970's. This crisis was also the killing blow for a large part of the Norwegian tankship fleet.

Reconstruction also provided a significant number of work places in the housing and construction industry. It wasn't just the rebuilding of houses that had been destroyed in the war that demanded large amounts of material and manpower. In addition there was the fact that home construction had been at a dead halt during the five war years, while the demand for housing had been increasing. This has meant that the lack of housing, nationally, was not remedied before 1980.

Many rivers have been tamed for electricity, but not the river Namsen which is a good place for fishing salmon.

Black gold

JOAN: Although North Sea oil is the most visible reason for Norway's current success and wealth, it is the growth of more traditional – but new and modern – industries that will maintain the nation into the 21st Century. The political leaders, economists, analysts, continually tell the people that the income from oil must be carefully spent in order to build traditional industries, and to find new industry, to fit the future.

An ongoing problem is the honest, often entirely too idealistic and blind, desire to protect and subsidize older industries, some steadily losing money, in order to protect jobs. Voter pressure, plus genuine caring, has caused many mistakes and cost the nation funds which could have been spent to build up new and viable industry for the future.

But it was oil that gave this small country of just over four million the essential boost it needed to get back on its feet. There are many oil companies in Norway today, but the story of just one of them is the story of the adventure.

An almost lost chance

JOAN: "One can disregard the possibilities of finding oil, gas or sulphur in the continental shelf along the Norwegian coast."

This was the judgement handed down by the Norwegian Council for Geological Research prior to the ocean rights

▷ The impossibly long pipeline was laid in record time, without incident. These gas pipes connect Gullfaks and the Statfjord Field with the West European gas network via Kårstø, in Rogaland.

◁ Drilling for «Black Gold.»

All construction in the North Sea is measured against the «hundred year wave», the biggest wave which might come in a hundred years. In September, 1979, a hurricane blew at Statfjord A, but the «hundred year wave,» which is measured at 28 to 32 meters, did not hit. ▷

conference in Geneva. Geologists had examined Norway and said, positively, there was no oil on land: Norway's geology is more than 600 million years old. Oil and gas are found in "younger layers" – layers no more than 300 to 400 million years old. And in the Norwegian trench, deep below the ocean? Impossible, said many. Norway's coast, underwater, resembles the coast above water. Just as the mountains on land appear to leap from the sea into the sky, so the land falls precipitously away into deep trenches in the ocean.

When the ocean rights conferences were held in Geneva in the 1950's it was advocated that the right of coastal nations to the offshore seabed should be on the condition that the seabed was a natural continuation of the topography which continued beyond the shoreline. Jurisdiction was not to be extended beyond the water depth where commercial exploration of mineral resources could be technically achieved – about 200 meters at that time. By this definition Norway would not own the seabed beyond the Norwegian trench. Britain's extension into the ocean sloped politely, evenly, out into the North Sea, as did Germany's, Holland's and Denmark's. It seemed logical to divide the North Sea between these nations and leave Norway on its side of the trench contemplating the dark fathomless depths.

Lucky decision

JOAN: Fortunately it was decided in 1964 that the Norwegian trench was an "accidental geological crevice," and therefore Norway should have its fair share. The boundary line was established at a midpoint between nations. In 1962 gas was discovered in Holland and oil companies began to look with interest at

Paper production is an old Norwegian industry.

other areas of the North Sea. In 1962 Trygve Lie, former Secretary General to the United Nations, and in 1962 serving as an Ambassador in the Norwegian Ministry of Foreign Affairs, told two representatives from Phillips Petroleum who were interested in exploring for oil off Norway, "I believe you must have made a mistake. Norway has no oil or gas."

In spite of such widespread skepticism, by 1964 some 17 oil companies had been granted rights by Norwegian authorities to do seismic work in Norwegian waters. Among these was Phillips Petroleum, America's eighth largest oil company, with its headquarters in Bartlesville, Oklahoma. Out of Texas and Oklahoma the oil men came, from homes where dust swirled through deserts and water was a precious rarity. Former cowboys, accustomed to battling sagebrush and heat, joined hands with Norwegian sailors, more accustomed to handling a fishing line than mammoth drills.

Ekofisk was discovered in 1969. By 1971, only 18 months after the Ekofisk discovery, Norway became an oil-producing nation. Phillips Petroleum, as operator for the Phillips Norway Group, has developed the seven Ekofisk oil and gas fields with its 22 manned platforms. Total investments in Ekofisk exceed six billion dollars – and the daily production of Ekofisk gas and oil represents more than twice Norway's daily consumption.

Oklahoma's Phillips Petroleum became Norway's biggest single taxpayer. Other American companies came to Norway and as the activities began to move north these were joined by oil companies from Great Britain, France and Italy. Norway's own company, Statoil, became the child prodigy of the oil industry. Norsk Hydro, once famous primarily for fertilizer, developed quickly into an oil business. Saga Petroleum became the third Norwegian oil company.

It's no longer fishing and shipping alone – today Norway exports skills and equipment in fields as advanced as electronics and computers.

△ Traditional industry, such as the Tinfos iron works, spewed out smoke and pollutants. Millions of kroner have gone into improvements at Tinfos to clean up the pollutants.

◁ Mangan, the Sauda foundry.

A life saver

JOAN: The oil industry provided an interesting partial solution to the growing problem in remote sections of Norway where work had declined. Small towns had been threatened with extinction as jobs disappeared. But the oil adventure allowed the Norwegian working on the field in the North Sea to stay in his remote village and not relocate his family. Work on a North Sea oil field is done in on-off stretches. Families could stay in well-loved areas of Norway that might have become ghost towns if the oil had not become a reality.

But the proud Norwegians were not about to let the Americans, nor any other nation, take control of "their" oil and gas. The Norwegians set about learning the business and proved adaptable and quick. In the astonishingly short span of years between 1969 and 1985 the number of Norwegians working at Phillips Petroleum in Norway grew from a handful to 96 percent of the total work force.

In the field of oil and gas exploration and development Norway has made some of the most exciting and important advances to be found anywhere. In the Spring of 1985 the underwater pipeline, bringing gas and oil from the North Sea fields to land in Norway, was completed – ahead of schedule. It was a feat many said couldn't be accomplished:

laying a pipeline stretching 850 kilometers across the ocean's floor and even across the Norwegian trench.

Endless riches?

JOAN: Those who said the petroleum flow would end in 20 years or so are beginning to realize their bleak forecast simply isn't so. Oil and gas are being found further north and new technology is going to enable it to be recovered without building elaborate rigs. Remote-controlled, unmanned, ocean bottom wells are now ready to be put into service in ever deeper waters in the inhospitable, far northern seas.

ARVID: Early 1986 two things happened that over night made the dream of oil less rosy. Firstly the price of oil on the international market fell to one third, from more than $30 to $10 a barrel. The consequence was a loss in state revenue of 35 to 40 billion kroners (app. $6.5 to $7 billion) for 1986.

Secondly approximately seven hundred catering workers in the North Sea went on strike. They claimed a wage hike of 30 per cent. The companies answered with lockout for all production workers. The conflict was long lasting and costly.

JOAN: What the oil has accomplished is to make the consequences of other, failing, businesses less generally felt. One of the ironic causes of the failure of older businesses is the rapidly rising standard of living and the demand by workers for a wage that is better than the industry can support.

If the oil workers earn a splendid salary, then the miner wants a similar salary – it's only fair. The fisherman knows he works as hard as the roustabout and sees his profit margin dwindling.

Free enterprise

JOAN: For all that the country is called socialist, free enterprise and impressive rewards for the enterprising are not rare. In a small town on the southwestern coast one young man turned a passion for wheels into a factory making wheelbarrows for farmers and from that into a multinational company making cranes and other transportation equipment, robots and, of course, wheelbarrows.

Nils Underhaug had a boyhood passion for cars and had built his first homemade automobile by the time he was 17. It was a 1.5 horsepower contraption riding on four bicycle wheels and noisy enough to scare all the neighboring farmers and livestock. Underhaug was a born wheeler-dealer.

In 1941 he opened his first factory to manufacture non-motorized transportation, with a start capital of 10,000 kroner saved from taking passport photographs and cutting turf. With two men helping he began

To be a fisherman is physically demanding. ▷

Oil threatens fishing – and fishing is the traditional lifestyle. Here brisling are being netted at Eidfjord, Hardanger. The fear of a serious oil spill is constant. ▽

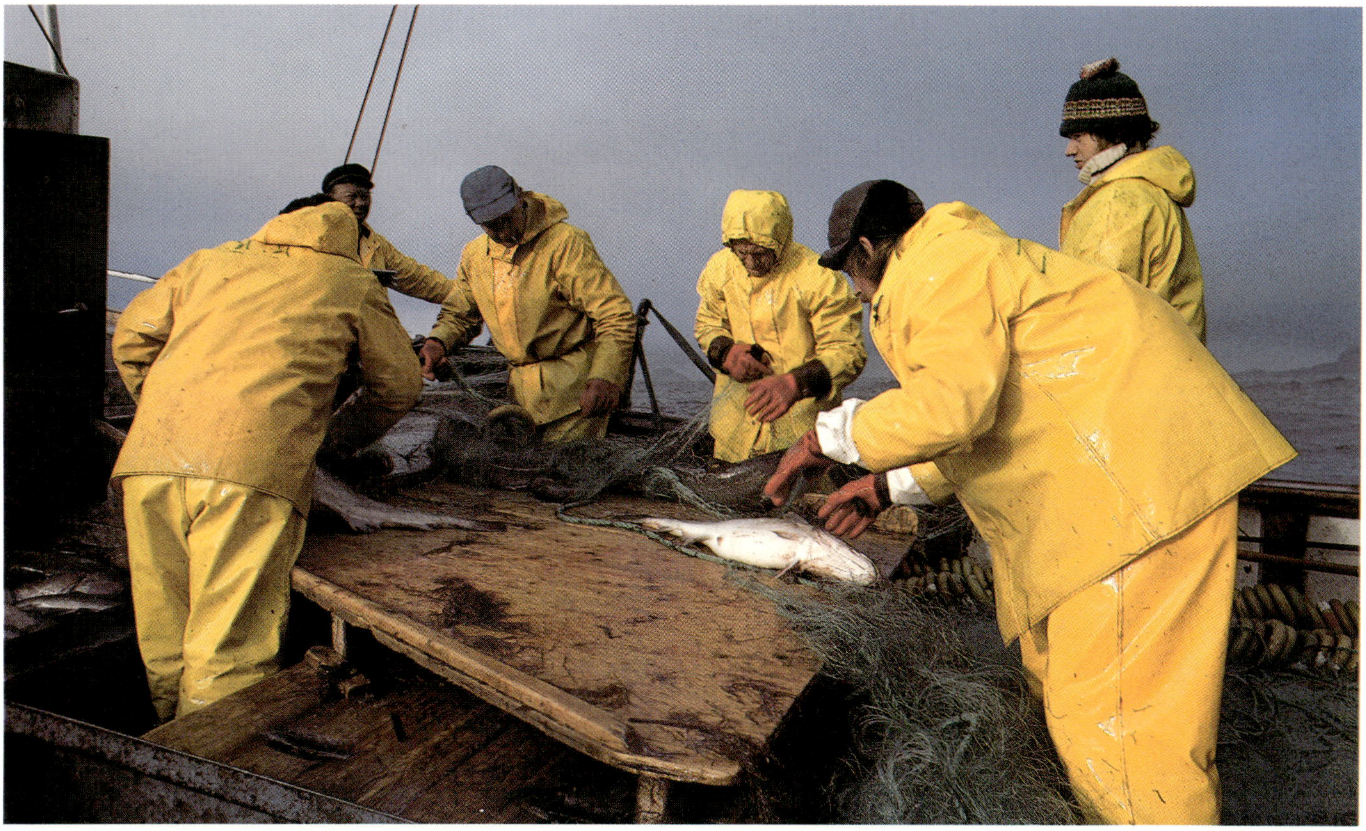

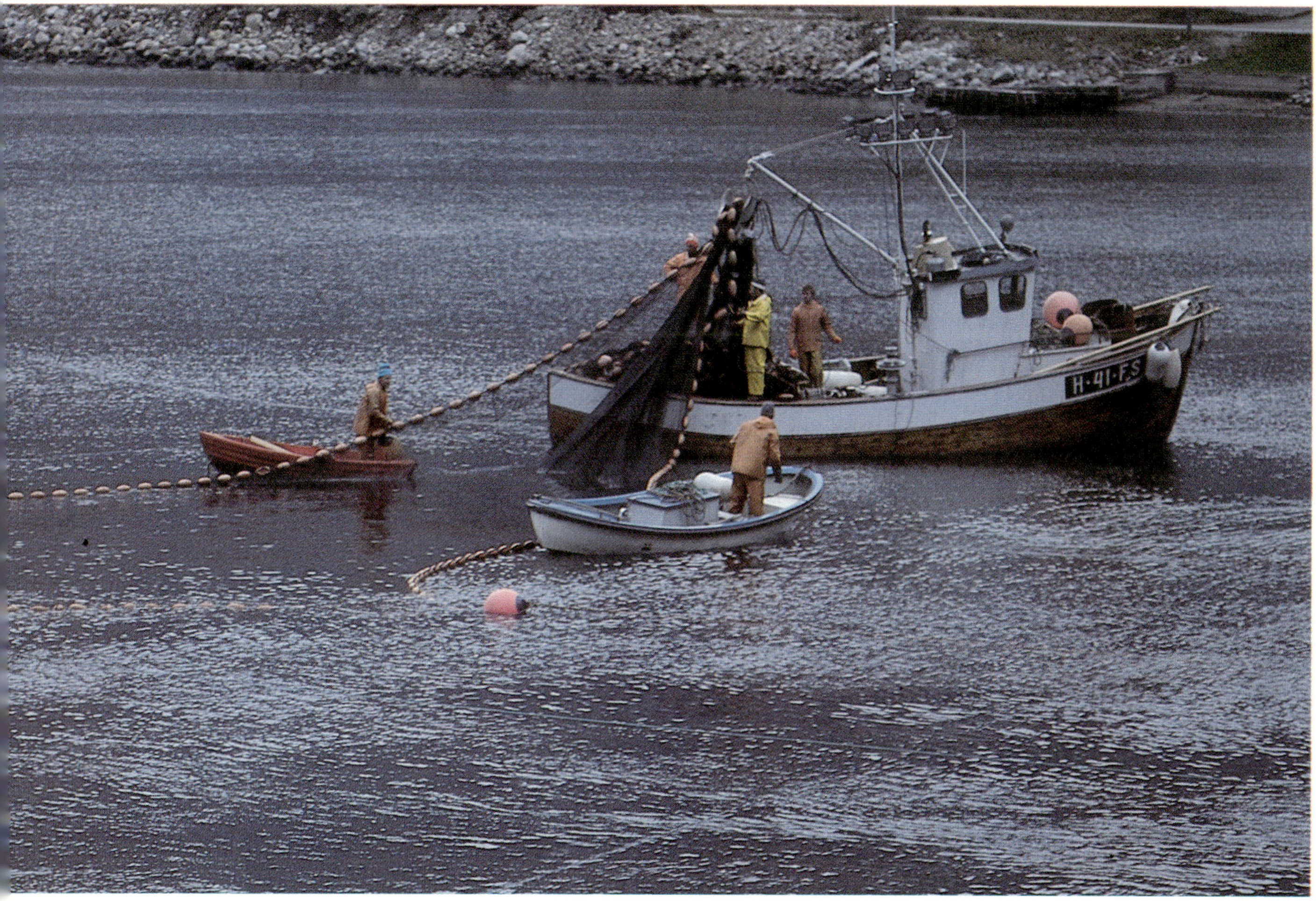
H-41-FS

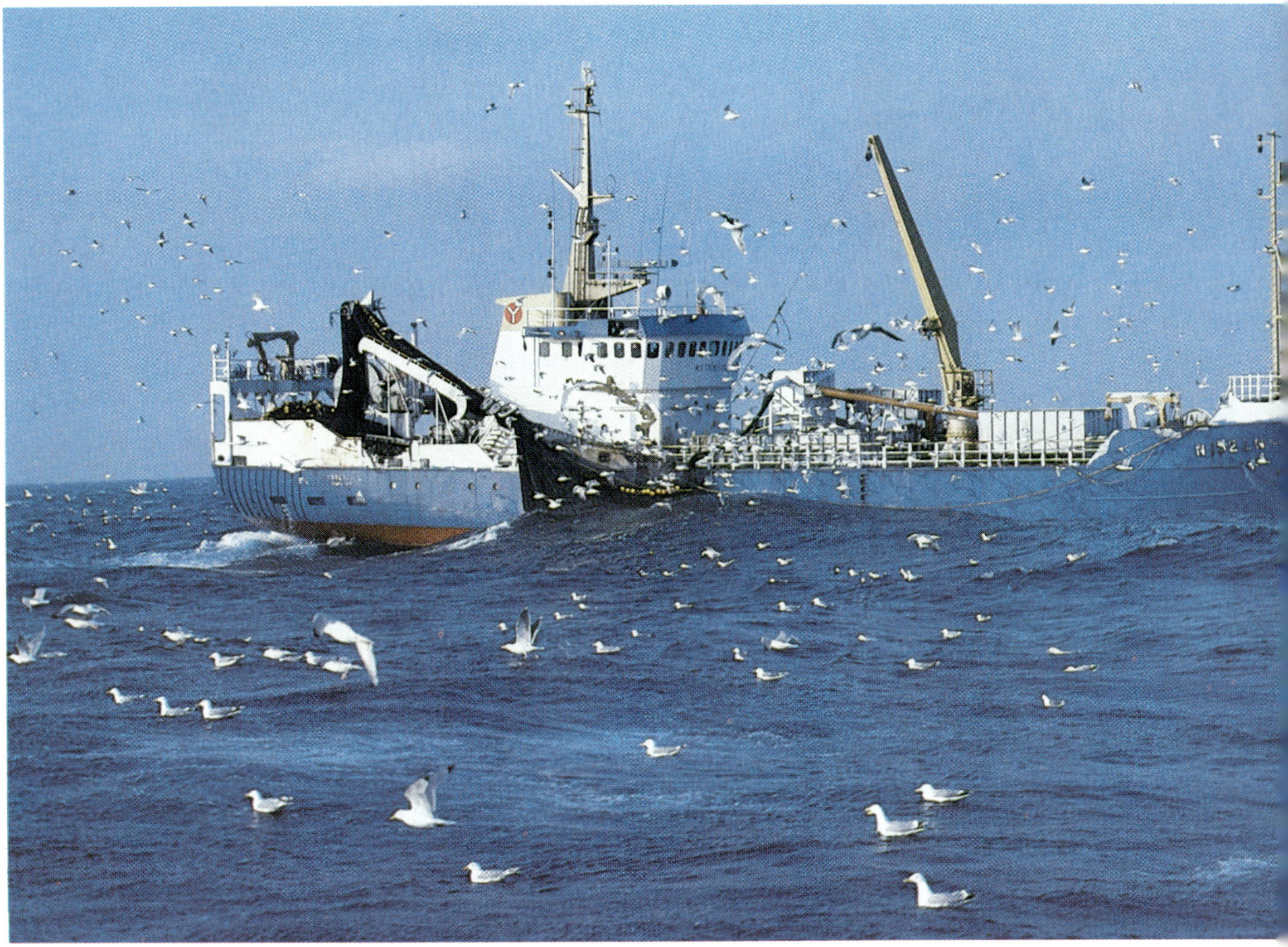

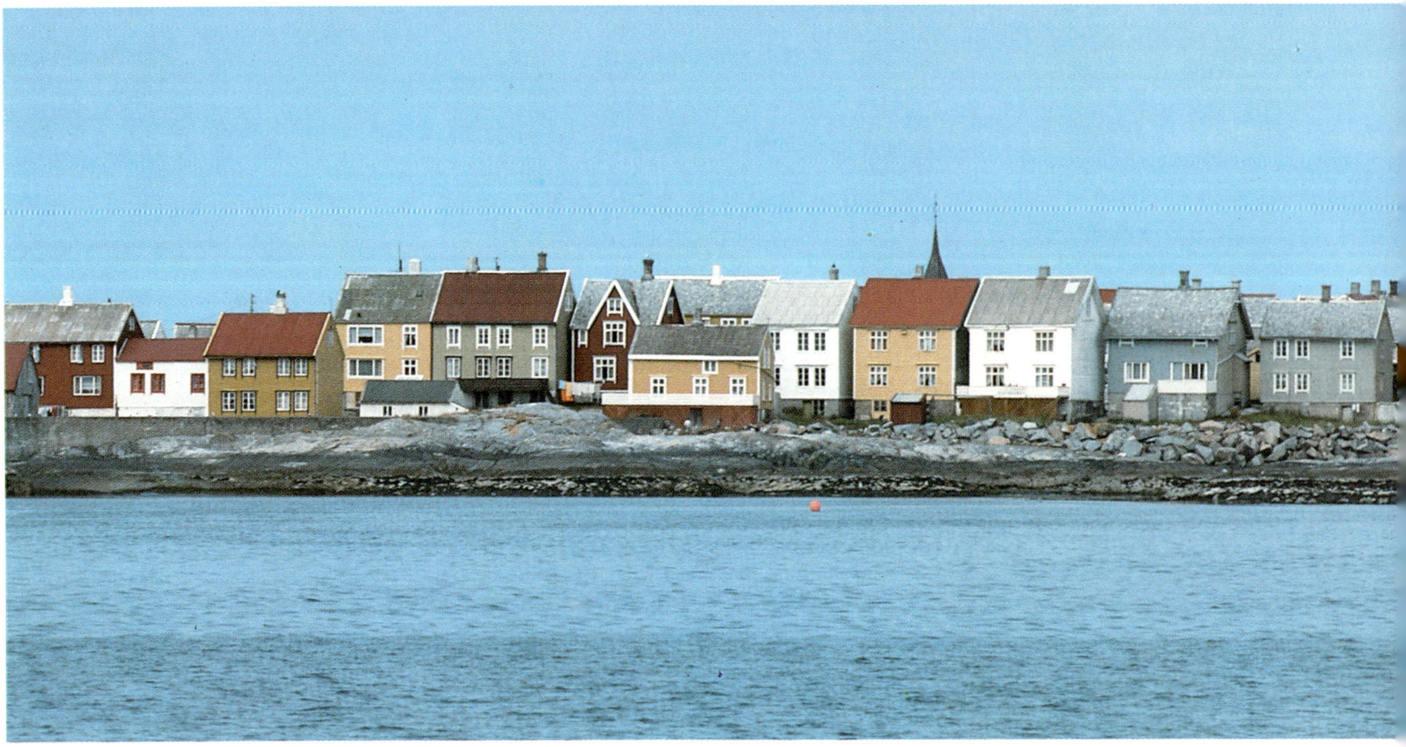

◁ Modern fishing has been industrialized and made more pleasant. But it is not always as idyllic as this.

▷ Island off Kristiansund: one of the fishing villages that has become a summer vacation spot.

▽ This is capelin, which is turned into fish flour.

producing his wheelbarrows, packingcarts, pushcarts and trailers to carry loads.

Even a jack-of-all-trades like Nils Underhaug could never have guessed that by 1984 his company, Trallfa, would have activities in Norway, Sweden, West Germany, England, Malaysia, Japan and the USA. What began as a wild venture into wheels has become a 140 million kroner business ('83) making hydraulic work platforms, industrial robots, snow removal equipment, carts, and of course 250,000 wheelbarrows.

A wet adventure

ARVID: Every day over the past two or three years, it has been possible to meet large refrigerator trucks on the way from Norway to airports in Sweden, Denmark, West-Germany, and even as far away as Great Britain. They are bringing fresh salmon and trout which is to be exported to the USA, and lately to Japan. The international flight capacity of airports within Norway cannot begin to reach levels which satisfy the demands from abroad.

Fish have always been important for Norway's economy, since the first hunters settled here more than 7,000 years ago. My mother's father rowed out to fish herring, from a farm in Ryfylke to fishing fields north of

Bergen. He and his five colleagues in that open boat were gone for six to eight weeks at a time. They sailed, and if there wasn't any wind, they rowed. At night they beached the boat and slept under it. It wasn't exactly first class quarters, particularly when the wind came from the north with snow and freezing temperatures.

Women, too!

JOAN: While the men were out weeks at a time fishing, the women did the farming with primitive tools, milked the cows, churned the butter and made the cheeses, canned the vegetables and preserved the fruit they'd handpicked. The women carded the wool from their own sheep and wove the clothes everyone in the family wore. They raised four, five, six children – often on those isolated farms we still see today perched on mountainsides out of reach of the rest of the world.

My corner grocery store owner told me of his mother's death in Ryfylke: "She raised eight of us on a farm while my father fished for a living. She worked a 16 to 18 hour day and even when she sat down to rest her aching legs and back she had something in her hands to work on. But since she died when she was only 75 I guess you could say she worked herself to death. She was too tired to live any longer." He actually said, "only 75."

When the Vikings roared out of Norway to attack England one thousand years ago they received all the publicity available from the only scribes of the time – the monks and priests in the monasteries, abbeys and churches they plundered. There were no literate monks around to write about the Viking women who were managing to protect Norway from invasion, do all the farming, husbandry, and raise children while the Viking men went a-raiding.

ARVID: My grandfather would undoubtedly stare at me in bewilderment if I had told him that the most important happenings in the Norwegian fishing industry today were aquaculture, fish-culture or fjord-farming.

Today's modern fishermen do not need to go out in a boat, they don't even need to wear boots when they want to go out after the day's catch. For they have their Atlantic salmon or the saltwater rainbow trout right there in fenced-in areas deep inside the fjord. The fish are cared for like other livestock: with the water, circulation and temperatures carefully regulated. Fjord-farming is the new industry experiencing the most explosive growth along the entire coastline.

Up to now it has been salmon and trout that have been most successfully farmed, but successful experiments are being made with other types of fish. In the experimental stage a cod has grown from sixty grams to four kilos in a nine-month period. Yearly production from

Humans aren't very big measured against the giant oil platforms.

Norwegian fjord-farming is now at around 25,000 ton, and stronger growth is expected in the years to come. Traditional ocean fishing has gone through a difficult period because of over-fishing by all the nations fishing in the North European ocean areas. A number of varieties of fish, such as herring, have been completely protected for a long time because of the dangerous decline in the species. The regulations have shown results and the herring are returning.

There are only 17,000 persons who claim fishing as their source of income today. This is a dramatic decline, compared to a few years back. Better equipment and ships have, in the meantime, led to an increase in productivity. Today some two million ton are fished, a total which has been constant for several years. But half of this is capelin, a small fish from the salmon family which is primarily used for fish powder.

The fisheries also provide jobs for some 80,000 persons on land, processing the products.

The new, super-effective, factory ships which vacuum the ocean for fish, and the pirates abusing the method, have created problems for all the fishing nations. Because of the establishment of the 200 mile economic zone Norway is much better off than most of the other nations.

JOAN: Fish flour, an almost waste by-product of the fishing industry, is becoming the hottest new health food item on the world market. There are claims that it cures everything from migraine to old age and people like me take a heaping tablespoon every morning.

The fish powder was used as a fertilizer for years, and was also used as a veterinary cure for animal ailments. Then the World Health Organization discovered it was an admirable cure for malnutrition in under-developed lands – particularly since it was dirt cheap.

I swear by fish flour – but I'm a closet neurotic and many people can't stand it in powder form, since it tastes like a combination of hay and cod liver oil. Nevertheless fish powder in tablet form is selling fast, and is sure to sweep the American market.

Capelin, the tiny fish Arvid talked about, is never eaten by Norwegians. But the funniest sight on television recently was Norwegians dressed up in kimonos going through elaborate Japanese ceremonies as they transferred a capelin catch to Japanese buyers. It seems the roe of the capelin is thought to have magical properties over potency in Japan. And now capelin roe is being sold in Norwegian stores – it wasn't to be found here in 1977. (Although I'm told it has been a delicacy in some parts of Norway.)

To me it looks as if the Norwegian fishing industry is on the brink of an enormous turn-around, and is another potential gold mine. Oil and fish – the products of the sea. It looks as if this is where Norwegians will make their fortune tomorrow, just as they are today, and as they have since the beginning of time.

POLITICS IN A WELFARE STATE

JOAN: "Vi har det så bra i Norge." "We have it so good in Norway."

Depending upon the age, political inclination and cynicism of the speaker, this phrase has various shades of semantic meaning. Still, everyone says it, and for the most part it is true. Norway is called a "Welfare State." What the majority of Norwegians really want is a welfare state tempered by a good portion of free enterprise.

This was conclusively proven when the Conservative Party, the largest non-socialist political group, was voted into power in 1981. There were brief periods in the 1960's when non-socialist parties took control – largely over the issue of Common Market membership – but until 1981 the socialist Labor Party had a majority of approval which dated back to the days of the depression.

Want it both ways

JOAN: But the classical socialist conflict, of the government acting as a benevolent protector versus an "every-man-for-himself" attitude has accelerated as the "good times" have become even better. Norwegians do not want to lose the benefits of a welfare state, they simply want the privilege of becoming independently wealthy.

This really isn't so unreasonable when it is understood that until recently Norway was so poor as to be "underdeveloped" by today's standards. The nation was so poor that Norwegians left Norway and emigrated in droves. In 1920 there were about 1.2 million people of "unmixed" Norwegian descent in the USA, or almost half the population of the motherland.

Good times

JOAN: By anyone's criteria Norway today "has it good." It enjoys one of the highest standards of living in the world. Unemployment is low, and the health services and social security system are well-developed. A democratic form of government and a separate judicial system ensure everyone a voice and protection under the law. The system is based on advanced ideals of equality and justice and these are clearly spelled out in legislation. Everyone has the right to employment, a place to live, an education, social security and hospital services. It is prohibited to discriminate against anyone on the basis of race, religion, political conviction or sex. Commissioners have been appointed to look after public administration, equal status and the conditions under which children and adolescents grow up. A great deal of money filters through the tax and social systems from those who earn the most to those who need assistance. The result is a society in which – at least theoretically – there are no extremes of poverty or riches.

The opening session of the Storting, with the Royal Family in attendance. Prime Minister Kåre Willoch, who leads a coalition government, addresses the gathering.

17th of May

ARVID: Norway celebrated its 1100th birthday in 1972. It wasn't a completely historically correct date: for 400 years we were under Danish rule, and we weren't counted as anything more than a Danish province. Fortunately for Norway the Danish king backed the wrong horse during the Napoleonic wars and the Englishmen patrolling the ocean between the two countries made Danish control over the colonies impossible.

Inspired by the American and French revolutions, we had our own in 1814. It was very peaceful, and consisted of calling a constitutional convention which declared that Norway was a free, indivisible kingdom. It gave us a constitution which is still usable today.

The constitution was signed on May 17, in Eidsvoll, north of Oslo. This date is still the day most celebrated in Norway. It isn't celebrated, as independence is in other lands, with military parades and displays of the most terrifying weapons, but by party-clothed children who walk in a parade and sing. In Oslo the children's parade always walks in front

△ The painting behind Kåre Willoch shows the Eidsvoll gathering of 1814 when Norway's Constitution was written.

In the old days families were larger, as can be ▽ seen in this painting «Afskeden» (The Departure) by Adolph Tidemand.

King Olav is «regular fellow», and even a cat can get his attention.   ▷

of the palace where the king and his family happily greet them and are in turn cheered. There are children's parades not only in every city but in every village. Children in the national costume, or in party clothes, can be seen walking between meter high snow banks, celebrating in their own way that we are an independent and freedom-loving people.

No sooner had the first Storting, in 1814, elected a Danish prince as the first king of the new independent Norway, than the Swedish King, Karl Johan, declared Norway was his. He was the former Marshall Bernadotte, Napoleon's officer, who in the meantime had become the King of Sweden. In his new country he chose not to support his former commander and therefore ended up on the winning side when Napoleon lost.

Norway had no way to resist and had to submit to the more powerful force. Nevertheless, in name, the country became an equal partner in a personal union. This lasted until 1905 when Norway had finally had enough of a union with the Swedes, and the Storting said, "stop, that's enough." There was mobilization on both sides and the danger of war was very real. But after a hectic period of diplomatic negotiating the tense situation was relieved.

This was the last time there has been anything like a serious conflict in the Nordic countries, and since then Nordic cooperation has grown in scope and importance and has been an important factor in each of the countries' politics.

The King

ARVID: The head of state in Norway is the King. He has only symbolic power and functions most of the time as a representative. Since the country became independent in 1905 we've had two kings: Haakon VII, and his son, Olav V. Both have, by their intelligent approach and

independence from any political parties, played an important role as national symbols of unity.

Particularly important was King Haakons clear "no" to the German occupation forces, and its Norwegian adherents, in 1940. The King and his staff moved to Great Britain and led the Norwegian resistance from London. The then Crown Prince Olav, who is now king, was commanding officer of the Norwegian forces, not because he was the king's son, but as a result of his military competence.

Repeated public opinion polls show that 84-year-old King Olav is Norway's most popular person. In his youth he was an active ski-jumper and has jumped at Holmenkollen. He has also taken an Olympic gold medal in sailing. He is still actively sailing, and despite his advanced age is among the best in the world. On a ski outing in Nordmarka in Oslo on a Sunday morning, it was always possible to meet the King and his small poodle going along in fine style in the forest. "I don't need security guards. I have four million Norwegians who watch over me," he once said to a foreigner who marveled that the King had no guards around him.

In the Norwegian constitution it still says that the king chooses his cabinet, government, and makes the decisions he thinks best. But in practice he is dependent upon a majority in the Storting when it comes to choosing a new government. And it is the government which decides what decisions the king should express.

Only males can be heir to the kingdom, but powerful forces are working to change this and do away with discrimination. As the situation is today, however, it is Crown Prince Harald (born in 1937) who will be Norway's next king and his son, Prince Haakon Magnus (born in 1973) is next in line.

The king cannot be charged in either local or national courts for anything done as a public or a private person. Norwegian law also has very strict penalties for any violence or attack on the king. Fortunately these two laws have never had to be invoked.

The Norwegian people aren't concerned with "blue blood." When Crown Prince Harald chose to marry a Norwegian commoner, Sonja Haraldsen, instead of a European princess, it was accepted as a matter of course, and Crown Princess Sonja is as popular today as any other member of the royal house.

The political system

ARVID: The one thing which has run through the Norwegian political system in the years since 1945 has been stability and agreement on the political goals, whether pertaining to foreign policies or internal matters.

Two important factors united the forces: the necessity to rebuild the land after five years of war and destruction, and the need to insure that Norway would never again be invaded and occupied by a foreign power.

As in most of Europe the political party system in Norway began with a liberal and a conservative party, left and right. These parties were formed in 1884 and 1885. From then and until the 1930's there were a number of splinters from the liberal party: the Farmer's party and The Christian Democrats in the center and Norway's Social Democratic Party which then later split again into the Labor Party and the Communist Party on the left.

In the years following WWI the Labor Party strengthened. The first Labor Party government was formed in 1928, but only lasted 19 days. In 1935 the party was back in power and it held power, uninterrupted, until 1963. During the five war years the government acted in exile from London.

Occupied Norway

ARVID: On April 9, 1940, the same day as the Germans began their massive invasion of this very poorly defended land, the leader of the National Assembly (NS), Vidkun Quisling, said in a radio broadcast that he had formed a "national government" with himself as Prime Minister and Foreign Minister. The party he headed had never been represented in the government and had only a few scattered members.

Both in Norwegian and in English the word quisling immediately became a synonym for traitor. Ideologically the party he led was related to Hitler's National Socialist Party. It advocated, among other things, the superiority of the Aryan race and participated actively in persecuting the Jews and in terror against the Norwegian civilians who passively or actively worked against the occupation forces and their Norwegian collaborators.

The Germans in Norway capitulated on May 8, 1945. The Norwegian king and government could again take over a land which was partly burned, where the social machinery and the financial system was either ruined or in a state of chaos.

The war had cost the lives of 10,000 Norwegians. Nine thousand Norwegians had been prisoners in German concentration camps. Many did not survive. Many came back damaged for life. Of the 760 Norwegian Jews who were sent to Germany, only 24 survived.

Two months after the war's end, almost 14,000 Norwegians were in jail, accused of treason. Thirty-seven persons, including 12 foreigners, were sentenced to death and executed.

One of the first to be executed was Vidkun Quisling.

This is the way Norwegians see themselves: a peaceful people with happy children and roots in nature's idylls.

From "broken rifle" to NATO

ARVID: Einar Gerhardsen, Labor Party leader who was Prime Minister in 1945 and for the next 20 years, went around in his youth with a broken rifle emblem on his jacket. The symbolism was clear: get rid of weapons. Gerhardsen was also arrested and jailed for having agitated as a conscientious objector.

It was a man with this past who led the greatest build-up of the Norwegian defense in history and who had the decisive vote when Norway joined NATO in 1949.

Gerhardsen was not the only Norwegian who, in the years between the two world wars, worked actively against the military. He had many sympathisers in many parties. For him and for the others the years of Hitler and the occupation, with its terror, murder and suffering, were the turning point. Therefore it was taken for granted in 1945 that the military should be strengthened in a responsible manner.

At the same time everyone realized that Norway alone would not be able to defend itself in a conflict. The first and most natural alternative was the security which membership in the United Nations gave. Norway had endorsed the UN convention in San Francisco in 1945 and believed, as did many other nations during the peace celebrations of 1945, that this international cooperation would provide a high degree of security, provided that there were no conflicts between the major powers which would limit the organization's negotiating strength.

From the Norwegian viewpoint this was particularly true since Norway's foreign minister, Trygve Lie, was the first Secretary General of the UN. But it wasn't long before tension grew, before Winston Churchill declared that "an Iron Curtain has descended upon Europe," and before everyone realized that the UN could not physically do anything to secure independence and integrity for the membership countries.

Norway's next alternative was a Nordic defense pact, to cooperate with Sweden and Denmark. The idea was first broached in 1947, and negotiations began, but nothing concrete came of it. A major reason against it was the Communist coup in Czechoslovakia in February 1948 which made Norway uneasy. This was hardly alleviated when Stalin, a short time later, insisted that Finland should sign a Finnish-Soviet friendship, cooperation and aid agreement.

Norway was then the only country with a common border with the Soviet Union which did not have such an agreement, and the Norwegian political leaders made it clear that we were in no way interested in such an arrangement. The result was that Norway and Denmark voted to go into NATO, while Sweden chose to maintain its neutral position.

Because of the strategic location of NATO's north flank, which has as its near neighbor the Soviet Union's largest marine base on Kola peninsula, Norway's defense is a higher priority matter today than ever before, both for the Norwegian authorities and the NATO chiefs.

△ Regularly NATO troops hold their combined winter maneuvers in Norway where the natural conditions test men and equipment.

Norway is a member of NATO, but there are ▽ Russians on Svalbard. The sign says: «A worker's collective is the best teacher.»

◁ Norwegian UN troops serving in Lebanon.

The Norwegian Coast Guard protects the territorial waters. ▽

The defense strategy calls for Norwegian forces to try to hold their position during the first critical days after a foreign attack and, as soon as possible, to receive help from the Allies. Norwegian policy clearly forbids placing nuclear weapons on Norwegian soil during peacetime.

Equal rights

JOAN: Norway was the first country in the world to grant full suffrage to women, in 1913. There is very little, in theory, left for women in Norway to fight for. In fact, however, they have battled so hard for their place in the work market that concerns such as special women's health needs have been neglected.

Norwegian men bend over backwards to be fair: they will stay home and do the housework so the women can go back to work; they can be seen every day walking the baby; there are absolutely none of the casual sexual put-downs or by-play games so very apparent in other countries; children spend much more time with their fathers here than in many countries. None of this has, however, helped lower the divorce rate. None of this has helped turn the "living together" arrangements into lasting relationships.

Being "fair" is one of the nicest of Norwegian characteristics and it pervades all of society. Homosexuals are receiving better treatment and noting a change of attitude. To me it seems as if the entire attitude to sex is "laid-back," relaxed and matter of fact. Abortion is upon demand and free, but decreasing in frequency. Norwegians tend not to talk about sex and this gives the foreigner the impression there isn't much. Wrong, wrong.

When I was new here I picked up a small box displayed by the check-out stand in the corner grocery and asked the checker, in all innocence, if it was

△ Shall we march for a shorter work week? Or perhaps for early retirement? All other major issues are long since settled, and Labor Day, May 1, doesn't attract the eager zealots it brought out 50 years ago.

▽ Since WWII new home construction has been unable to keep up with the demand.

◁ The welfare state has been successful in Norway.

stockings. It took a lot of explaining, and she blushed, but I finally understood it was condoms that were being displayed so openly.

Unmarried youngsters will often live together in a parental home. But since it is neither discussed nor viewed as particularly shocking, foreigners are hardly ever aware of it.

1st of May

JOAN: On May 1 every working person should be marching in the streets celebrating: it's the Norwegian Labor Day. A lot of work went into turning Norway into a social democracy. Certainly the worker's movement explains some of the attitude in this country that makes it almost impossible for Norwegians to take subservient jobs. They bowed and scraped once upon a time and they will not do so today.

But May 1 is a national holiday, and if the sun is shining most of the newly rich workers will be found fixing their boats, getting their cabins ready for summer – but not downtown parading. Today's Norwegian sees the parades as being for the Labor Party or the socialists or the communists, not for the center or right wing parties. This is, of course, a distortion of the original solidarity. But no matter how far right today's Norwegian thinks he/she is, they are still far to the left of most other nation's conservatives.

It could be said, today, that the tail (the union) is wagging the dog. For the newcomer this is astonishingly apparent in the large number of attractive buildings owned by the unions (complete with swimming pools and hotel attachments) and the long lists of courses, scholarships and stipends which are given out.

Unions – a power factor

ARVID: There's no place in the world where the unions have as much influence and as much power as in Scandinavia in general and in Norway in particular. In contrast to the way it has been in the USA, for example, the union movement here in Norway is acknowledged and respected. Almost all employers see the unions as a necessary, positive and stabilizing element.

Most workers in Norway are organized in local unions which are in turn part of larger groups, either the Landsorganisasjonen, which is politically allied with the Labor Party, or in independent unions which have no direct party affiliation. At the same time the majority of employers are joined together in a central organization.

The workers' biggest weapon is the strike. The employer hits hardest with a lock-out. It has been said countless times through the years that the strike and the lock-out do not belong in a modern industrialized society where the inter-dependence is vast and complicated. But neither of the parties are brave enough to act on the thought.

Unity is strength, was the slogan when workers joined to demonstrate in parades on May 1, and it is said today, despite the fact that many union members use the holiday to go to their cottages or fix up their boats.

Unity can most clearly be seen in the yearly wage negotiations which are held at a set time. Long before the deadline the worker's organizations make clear their demands which are based upon price developments, inflation and the general economic climate. Concurrently the employers make their offers. From these beginnings come the negotiations. If the two sides agree, the findings are voted upon by the union memberships. Only rarely are such negotiations rejected, but when it happens the result can be a strike or lock-out. If the conflict hinders activities vital to society the Storting can pass an order for compulsory arbitration,and call in a special arbitrator who has the power to bind both parties.

In this way the wage and fringe benefit packages have a similarity which insures against discrimination. In addition to these cooperative, central negotiations, there are local negotiations between the individual unions and the company. These can provide more money and extra fringe benefits to the individual worker.

The union's representatives are often accused of lacking responsibility and of not paying attention to the employer's particular

Many political demonstrations end up at the headquarters of the social democrats.

problems connected with competition or business cycles. This criticism has died down in recent years, and there must have been applause in the board room in 1985 when the major union said it was not going to ask for a wage increase. Previously the press has often been called the Fourth Estate, after the king and government and the judicial system. But shouldn't the unions be called the Fourth Estate and the press be shoved down to fifth place?

Another viewpoint

JOAN: An immigrant who has been in Norway long enough to fit into the system has the advantage of being more "aware" of the benefits and drawbacks in the Norwegian welfare programs than one who has grown up with them and knows no other way of life. If a foreigner is fortunate enough to get a job, some advantages are immediately awe-inspiring. This is a nation where everyone is entitled to four weeks paid vacation (five weeks in some positions where individual unions have negotiated five). These four paid weeks become five after the age of 60. The pay for these holiday weeks is tax-free and based either on the actual wage earned for the time or a percentage of the year's income, whichever is greater. Best of all, this vacation is for everyone, not just for those in top jobs, as in some countries. Even some farmers and housewives can demand, and get, paid vacations – with the government paying for their stand-ins. In addition to this there are at least two and a half days at Christmas and a minimum of five days at Easter. Then there are the additional holidays of Ascension Day, Whitsuntide Monday, May 1 and Constitution Day, May 17.

To a foreigner it is primarily vacations that illustrate how prosperous Norway is. Statistics show that two out of every three Norwegians planned a vacation trip away from home in the summer of 1985. Of these an astonishing number travel out of the country. Travel bureaus do a rousing business and are constantly coming up with new and more exotic destinations. Travel of this sort must be considered a luxury, one that would never be considered if the budget was tight.

Free coffee

JOAN: In most jobs there's free coffee available all day; workers are entitled to a window if they work steadily in one place. (This requirement makes for some very strange architecture and a good deal of expensive waste space.)

A worker with a doctor's or dentist's appointment gets paid time off with no questions asked and the paid time off usually extends also to appointments with physical therapists.

The law says the working hours are a maximum of nine a day, 40 a week. Individual unions, however, have brought the total down to 36 or 38 hours. Overtime is any time over the lawful limit and is paid for at a premium of at least 40% above basic pay. Overtime is strictly limited by law – no one may work more than 25 hours overtime in any consecutive four week period, nor work more than 14 hours any one day. If you work overtime on holidays your employer usually sends in catered meals!

There's practically nothing left for a union to get excited about. A fringe benefit negotiated for, and received, by a newspaper union recently included a suitcase for every reporter – to compensate for wear-and-tear on a reporter's luggage. Everyone tends to know what everyone else earns, which can be disconcerting to the new foreign worker accustomed to some privileged workers receiving much more than others. The "welfare" principle is that there should be little difference between bottom and top salaries. That this may have an adverse effect on ambition and willing-ness to put in extra effort is a problem the nation is only beginning to grasp.

Right to be sick

JOAN: The foreign worker, accustomed to being afraid for his job, is appalled to discover his Norwegian co-worker happily taking "sick leave" for something like a pulled muscle, and feeling absolutely no threat, no job insecurity. In addition to the days off for a doctor-excused health problem for themselves, the parents of small children are allowed a total of 20 sick days a year (ten each) to take care of ailing youngsters. All these

Norwegians live longer than any other people on▽ this globe. The birthrate is falling. Soon the grow-ing numbers of retired will threaten the welfare state.

They may not be born with skis on, but they put ▷ them on as soon as they can toddle, and go to skischool as soon as they are allowed and then, of course, begin to enter in competitions where – it is easy to see – everyone is a winner.

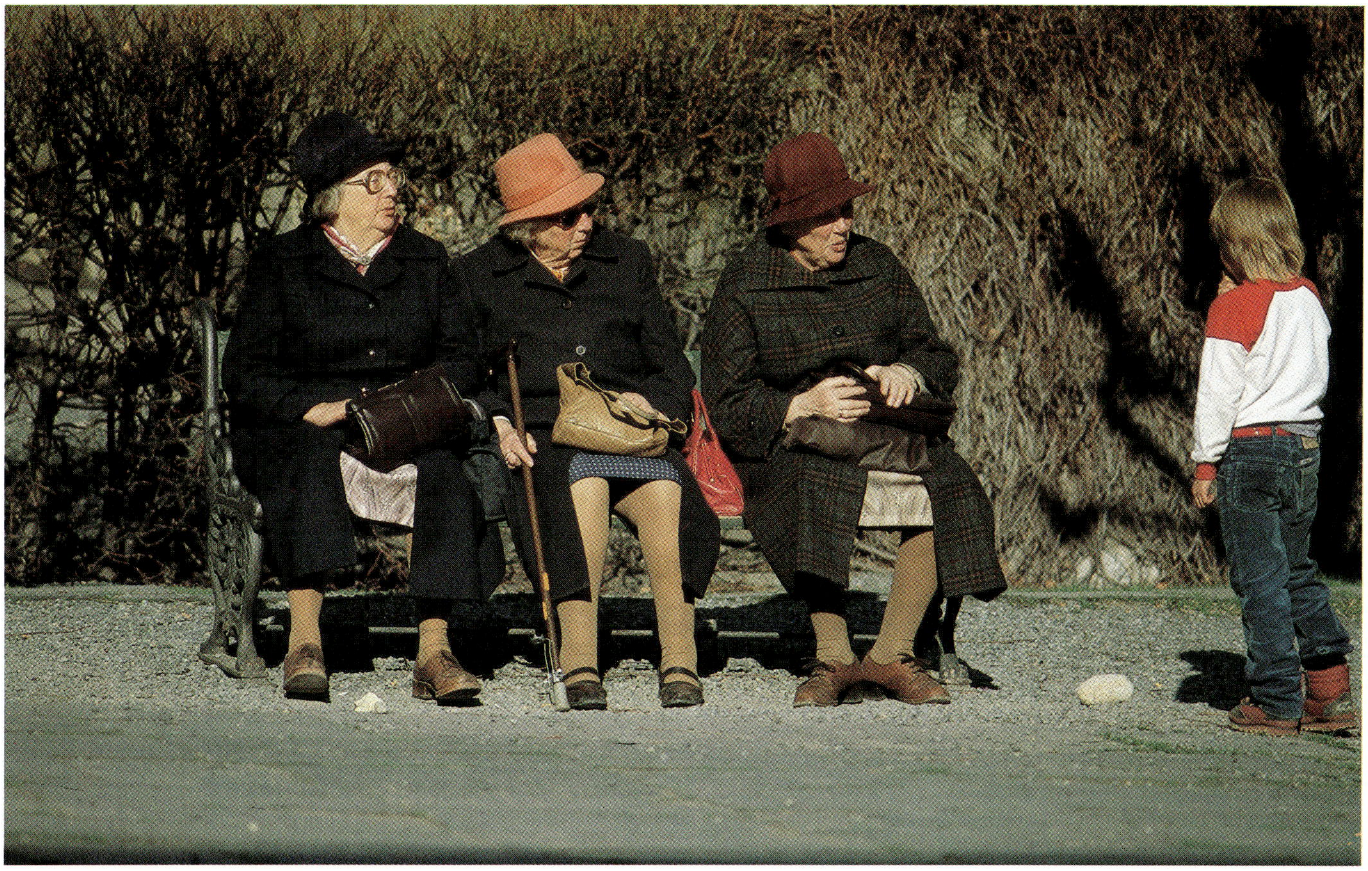

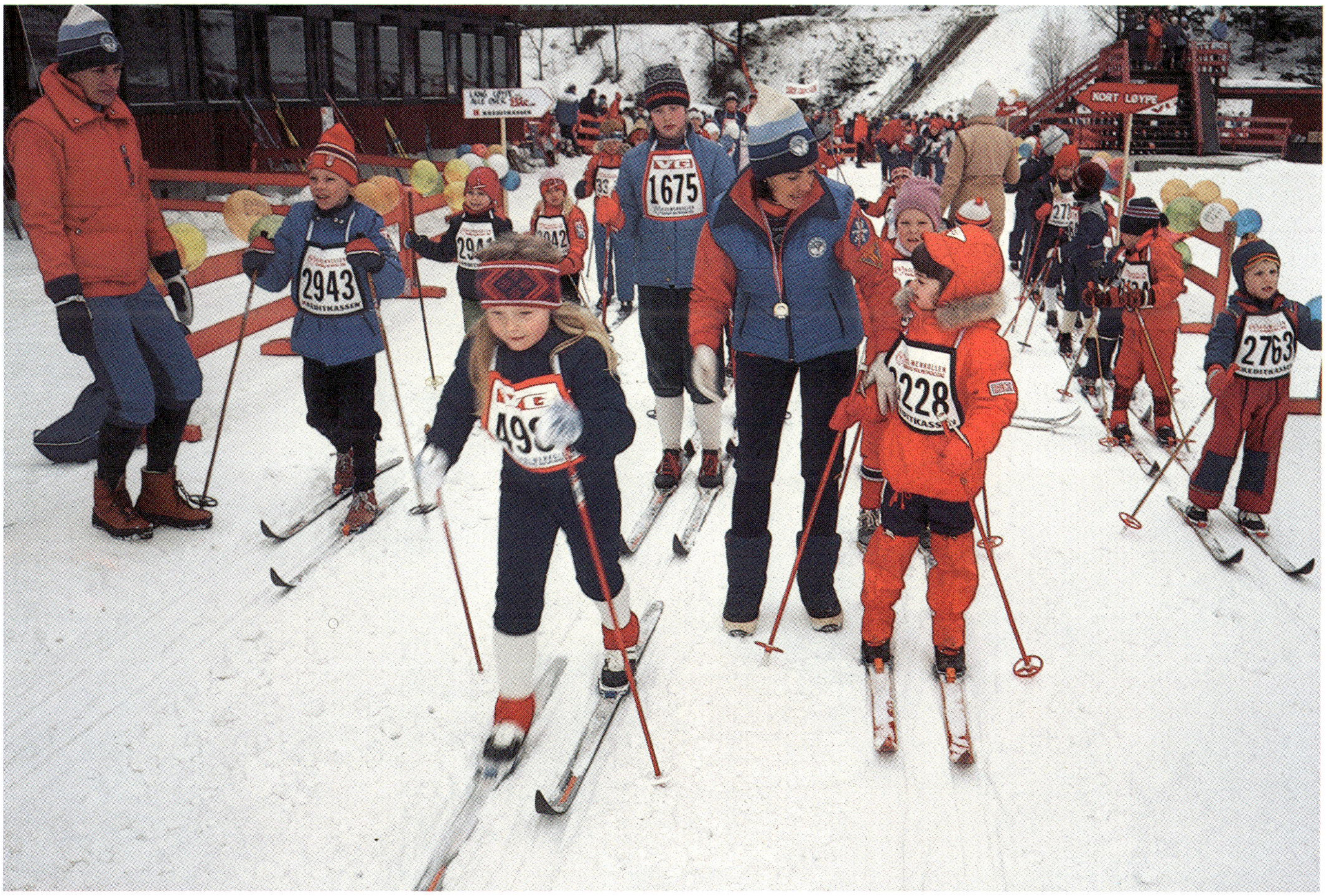

KORT LØYPE
2943
1675
2228
2763

with full pay of course. In the event of catastrophic illness, such as a heart attack, a worker is entitled to one full year at full pay.

Providing welfare in health and social services is where the system is cracking and may break wide open in years to come. Twenty years ago it could be said that socialized medicine worked perfectly when the people were too proud to be sick. Norwegians remembering the depression, the war, are still too proud to be sick and are pleased to have perfect attendance records. They grew up poor and are delighted to work. The younger generation feels no such pride. They feel they have worked for the privileges and they have a perfect right to their share of the benefits.

Additionally, the burden placed upon the medical system has increased proportionately with the improved services. The growing number of old people in a country with the highest life expectancy in the world multiplies the problems. Children receive free dental care. Most adults go to private practice physicians and pay a normal fee which is supplemented by government payments.

However the medical benefits picture is not rosy. There are long waits to see doctors, it can take months to get a referral and get to see a specialist, and there are inexcusably long waits for those needing elective surgery in regional hospitals. For instance it can take up to two years to receive orthopedic surgery.

One answer, of course, to the problem of inefficient socialized medicine, is private care. Norway's first private medical center opened May 20, 1985 in Oslo. Its director, Jens Moe, says Ring Medical Center is an alternative to the "cumbersome, expensive, State plan." It seems as if Norwegians were ready for an alternative plan since the full, initial quota of 3,500 subscribers was reached quickly.

Essential pharmaceutical drugs, for the treatment of chronic illnesses such as arthritis, high blood pressure, diabetes, cost a nominal fee with the government picking up the rest of the cost. Ordinary medicines, including pain medication and antibiotics, are paid for by the patient, with some categories of patients receiving refunds if their need is great.

Better than USA

JOAN: From the viewpoint of the newcomer that part of medical cost in Norway which is paid in through taxes seems no higher than the amount which was paid into private insurance in the USA. In addition there is an enormous sense of relief at knowing it is impossible for one sick family member's bills to wipe the family out financially – to bankrupt a family that was self-sufficient only months earlier. It is a system giving the individual an unusual sense of security because everyone receives equal care, with no questions asked as to personal financial status.

On the debit side, however, is the inexcusable lag between

Extraordinary efforts are put forth to take care of the individual, despite the health delivery problems. Coastal ships bring the sick to mainland hospitals, helicopter ambulances do heroic rescues.

consumer need and the answering medical service. Too many people wait too long for proper care and treatment. Acute, emergency care is excellent. The care received once one is admitted to a hospital is top rate. But preventive medicine is woefully behind what is needed. And, as in many countries, there is way too much bureaucracy behind the welfare.

Big Brother

JOAN: Big Brother – as expressed in a welfare state – can and often does "protect for the common good," until it feels as if the individual freedom is being sorely pinched. There are exorbitant taxes on cigarettes and alcohol – but these are "sinful" items. Automobiles are kept almost prohibitively expensive. Overtime work is taxed so highly that no one can be motivated to put in extra hours. This is to keep unemployment down and to make sure a person has the necessary free time.

What happens of course is that while motivation to work on the job is killed, there is plenty of motivation to earn "black money," money under the table and not taxed.

Norwegians want to live by socialist ideals but, being human, they want to fulfill their individual ambitions. That they are walking that tightrope quite successfully is largely due to the still prevailing Puritan work ethic.

Gambling fever

JOAN: The collective social conscience also extends into personal life.

The runaway most popular method of donating to charity is also most Norwegians' favorite pastime, almost a fever: lottery betting. The cancer society, heart fund, blind organization and every other charity raise their yearly quota by soliciting donations which are also chances in a lottery.

For ten kroner you can donate to a good cause and perhaps also win a new car, or a cottage, or a trip to a sunny beach in the South – tax-free. Gambling winnings obtained by the national lottery (Pengelotteriet, 20 kroner a chance, drawing twice a month), betting on the soccer pools, or donating to charity are all tax-free initially, which makes them all the more attractive. The national lottery provides much-needed funds for scientific research. The football pools raise funds to provide swimming pools, soccer fields and other sports opportunities. Gambling by lottery thereby satisfies the universal human need to hope for the "pot of gold," and at the same time does the most good for the most people. Eminently practical and realistic, these Norwegians. Or have they found a sensible way to justify what might otherwise have to be termed a "sin?"

Briksdals glacier.

CUSTOMS AND CULTURE

Cultural policies

JOAN: The welfare state concept works best in Norway, in my opinion, when it comes to encouraging individuality, cultural life and sports. The official Norwegian cultural policy is blessed with an attitude which doesn't just encourage protecting and exhibiting art, but also individual involvement and initiative. In 1984 the government set aside more than one billion kroner for cultural projects.

The longterm goal is to bring the artists' income up to the level of other groups', and the Norwegian artists association is the only one of its kind with negotiating rights. It is typical of Norway that this institution, which exists because of state support, is operated by the artists themselves.

The State guarantees for a minimum printing for fiction, and all books are exempt from sales tax. Subsidized funds are available to print Norwegian classics, publish modern drama, to arrange debut concerts, to artistically decorate buildings, to order musical compositions, and to print music and records. A good bit of money also goes to protect and promote Sami culture.

The emphasis placed on individual differences can be seen in the amazing amount of money which is given for school books and other general publications to be printed in at least two languages: bokmål and nynorsk, with many also printed in Sami.

The Sami came first

ARVID: The people that used to be called Lapps, from Lapland, have made it quite clear that they now wish to be called Sami. This name has officially replaced Lapp or Laplander, in all languages.

The Sami have been called Norway's Indians. The comparison is appropriate. As far as anyone can tell they were already established on what would become Norway when the first Norwegians came North. The oldest prehistoric archeological finds have been found in what was then Lapland. Just like the North American Indians the Sami lived in a society where ownership of property was unknown.

The Sami distributed the day's fishing and hunting yield to each family according to its need. Formerly the Sami were often defined by their appearance: they were short, with wide faces and high cheek bones. But you can also find Sami who are tall and blond.

The language has been another criterion. It is completely different from Norwegian and closer to Finnish. But physically and anthropologically there are great differences between Sami and Finns. And there are Sami today who cannot speak Sami. The Sami say that a person is a Sami if he identifies himself as a Sami.

Norway's capital, Oslo, is the largest Sami city in Norway, and you find Sami in authority, as newspaper editors (for "Norwegian" newspapers) and in many other prominent positions. Sami are to be found in Norway, Sweden, Finland and the Soviet Union, and it is

△ Raising reindeer demands large amounts of range land. This means driving the reindeer between the winter grazing lands inland to the summer grazing areas near the coast. In April the reindeer swim over the fjord to graze on an island, Magerøy. Reindeer are a way of life, fitting the natural area where they are found.

▽ The approximately 30 to 40 Skolte Sami, who are members of the St. Georg Chapel in Neiden, Sør-Varanger, meet for a Greek Orthodox ceremony.

◁ The Sami have been politically active in recent years in efforts to maintain the wilderness areas they treasure.

estimated there are between 30,000 and 50,000. Most live in Norway, where it is estimated the population is about 20,000. The Sami who are reindeer handlers, which is the stereotype from posters and is the way most people picture them, are a small minority of about 10 percent. Most Sami combine fishing and farming, or live inland on rivers in the primarily Sami towns of Karasjok, Kautokeino and Polmak. There are also the "Skolte" Sami, in South Varanger. They are Greek Orthodox and have their very special churches with icons and other decorations found nowhere else in Norway.

Zealous Norwegian missionaries tried hard to eradicate Sami cultural heritages. Until the last world war all education was in Norwegian. The Sami were discriminated against because they were Sami, and many became so confused that they didn't dare acknowledge their own language and culture.

Over the past twenty years there's been a consciousness raising among the Sami. Part of its solidarity has come from battling the Norwegian authorities over power stations and other controversial issues which have threatened traditional Sami areas.

JOAN: There were many injustices in the past that diminished the Sami culture, but in spite of this – or perhaps because of it – there are many noble and extra efforts today to right these wrongs. There are daily Sami news broadcasts. Television shows about the Sami in Norwegian will be subtitled in Sami. On a television show where both Norwegian and Sami are spoken, subtitling will be in both languages. The Sami have a rich and varied cultural life which receives more recognition yearly, while their unique and marvelous bone carvings have already become famous worldwide.

Norwegian national costumes

JOAN: As might be expected the Sami national costume is made of warm wool in the brightest of colors. They also have winterwear of reindeer skins and the women often wear cotton in the summer, as it can be very warm north of the Polar Circle.

National costumes over the rest of Norway are also made in strong colors, either in the material itself or in the embroidery. In winter, individual areas, valleys, and mountains would be totally cut off from outside contact. Many people lived and died without having gone more than one valley away from home. One obvious result of this is that Norway, today, is a nation with almost as many national costumes as there are areas, instead of just one as in other countries.

The costume (called "bunad") is, traditionally, embroidered wool with a white linen blouse decorated with embroidery or lace. You could tell the

△ Borgund stave church from 1150.

▽ Plays by Ludvig Holberg are popular from generation to generation. Here Erasmus Montanus shows he is educated enough to prove that «Mother Nille is a stone.»

◁ Anyone who can, will wear one or another version of the national costume – here in a wedding that could take place today, or could have happened 200 years ago.

married woman from the single woman only by the headdress. The "bunad" that stands out from all the others comes from the valley of Setesdal, north of Kristiansand. The people in this valley were more isolated than most, and it shows in the woman's "bunad," which consists of a short skirt, filled out with many ruffled petticoats. The "bunads" from other areas reach to the ankle.

The Setesdal "bunad" is also the most expensive to make as it is decorated all over with handmade silver ornamentation instead of embroidery. The Setesdal valley has always been famous for its silversmiths. Back in 1970 a Setesdal "bunad" for a man and a woman took two years to make by hand and cost an American collector $7000.

Most Norwegian women want a "bunad" because it is the only formal attire that spans seasons, styles, years. It is always appropriate and always admired. Since it is a lifetime investment it is cleverly made with an expandable waistband. The men's versions are simpler and not nearly as popular since they are not as adaptable to all social events.

Folk dancing

JOAN: Norwegian folk dancing comes in two variations. The original folk dances were the Halling, Spring and the March and are done by a small elite, only in bunad, and must not be confused with the other folk dance form, gammeldans. This is more widely popular and people of all ages take part with zest and according to individual ability. Many of these, like the Rhinelander, polka and waltz, came from other countries. Song dances originated in Norway, but are rather dull.

Individual valleys had a demanding dance called the Spring, which was, in effect, a test of a young man's ability. In the Halling a man does a great leap ever higher in the air to finally kick a hat off a pole. It is a dancing contest for men and the one who is the last to kick it off, with his heel, way up there in the air, is champ.

Theater today

JOAN: Theater has enjoyed a period of growth with five regional theaters having been established since the mid-1970's. Traveling troupes play in schools and barns in remote areas. Subsidies ensure that a theater ticket's price is kept reasonable. Television has had a beneficial effect on theater, bringing drama to a greater audience and in turn bringing the people out of their living rooms and into the theaters.

Theater is very well-attended and children's productions play to full houses. Although the Norwegian National Opera only celebrated its 25th anniversary in 1984, Norway has produced some of the most famous singers of our time, such as Kirsten Flagstad, Ingrid Bjoner and Ragnar Ulfung. The opera and the Opera Ballet have occasional tours around the country and bring music and dance to people living far from cultural centers.

Norway is also a foremost jazz nation with annual festivals in Molde and Kongsberg. Many of the country's own jazz musicians had their training in the school bands, the most widespread of all forms of musical experience. There are more school bands per capita in Norway than in any other country in the world, which indicates just how important music is at the grass roots level.

It is only in recent years, however, that professional music has received priority. The results have been spectacular. The Olso Philharmonic, under the direction of Mariss Jansons, has received international acclaim for its Tchaikowsky recordings, and is reaching top ranking among orchestras worldwide.

Several fine concert halls and cultural centers have opened in Norway in the last decade. The Oslo Concert Hall, the Grieg Hall in Bergen and Bjergsted in Stavanger are examples of attractive new buildings. Music, like all other institutionalized culture, is subsidized by the central, county and municipal governments with the State paying the greatest share.

The Bergen International Festival has been a major force in promoting Norwegian music and the superb Norwegian production of the Glenn Tetley/Arne Nordheim ballet based on Shakespeare's "The Tempest," had its debut at this popular May event on the west coast. Since then it has also been performed in the USA, to much acclaim.

Some artists, and writers, claim Norway is paradise: art sells. At the opening of an exhibit of work by a popular artist the crowd pushes through the door and the red "sold" marks appear before any viewer has really had time to study a work. It is actually possible to make a modest living as an artist in Norway and artists from other countries often settle here. Even small towns in the backwoods boast of at least one or two town statues: depicting founding fathers, other famous men and women, stylized romantic depictions of fishing, sailing, war heroes, or simply children and animals.

The popularity of art is also shown by the art clubs in many businesses. Employees pay a small monthly sum through payroll deduction. A committee of workers goes out and buys original artwork, and the work is distributed by chances drawn once a year. The lucky winner acquires art he/she could otherwise never have afforded.

The famous Gustav Vigeland

JOAN: Gustav Vigeland (1869-1943) was the first Norwegian sculptor to win international renown, and his major effort, the sculpture park in Oslo, is a prime tourist goal. Because Vigeland's nude statues are extremely earthy and sensual, Norway hesitated almost too long giving him recognition and came close to losing Vigeland to Sweden. But finally the authorities gave him his unique park which became a

Cultural centers have been built in several cities in recent years. This photograph shows the new Oslo Concert House at its opening ceremony in 1977.

spectacular monument to one superior artist's ability. He said the world must come to him, and it does. No reproductions are allowed.

Tourists make their way to Frogner (or Vigeland) Park – but all too few make it to the museum across the street. The museum was Vigeland's home and studio and in it can be seen plaster models of his superb ideas about the clergy, the devil and temptation.

The work of Gustav Vigeland illustrates just what unique and priceless gifts can be left to mankind when a talented genius is freed from financial worries and encouraged to produce the best possible work. Obviously this much freedom and encouragement for one artist can't occur often.

Writer's paradise

JOAN: Norway's primary indoor activity is reading. Norwegians read more than any other nation in the world, spending an average of 500 kroner a year, per capita, on books. More than 2,000 new titles are published annually and a total of more than 35 million books ran off the printing presses in 1984. Around 10 percent of these are novels, collections of short stories and books of poetry written by Norwegians. There is a public library in this country for every 2,500 to 3,000 people. In addition there are bookmobiles serving neighborhoods and book boats for the island communities. Besides all these there are 3,761 school libraries and 427 professional libraries (1983 figures).

An American writer may point to the small Norwegian population, and the use of an obscure Northern European language, and feel smugly superior. But the smug feeling changes to envy when the Norwegian writer tells of receiving royalty payments each time a book is checked out of a library anywhere in the country; or talks of receiving a government subsidy or an annual guaranteed income! The payment from library withdrawals is small, but it is paid regularly. In addition each and every one of the 1,373 public libraries in Norway is required to purchase each and every popular work published.

High educational level

JOAN: "Problems" are debated endlessly in Norway, no matter how obscure they may be. There is an enormous amount of awareness, thanks in large part to there being almost 100 percent literacy, and a high educational level. There are 165 newspapers published in Norway, 80 of which come out five or six times a week. Deep personal attachment to one's local area means that the local newspaper is a major force. More newspapers are published per capita in Norway than in most other industrialized countries. Most surprising of all is that

Graduating seniors are an important part of the May 17th celebrations. The about-to-be-adults in red are graduating from the academic school while those outfitted in blue have gone to commercial schools.

these newspapers are read from the first to the last page, down to the smallest advertisement.

Broadcasting

JOAN: Broadcasting, on the other hand, has been a monopoly for many years which is only now breaking down. Local radio stations arrived on FM in the early 80's and the television monopoly is threatened by the advent of satellites and cable. No advertising is permitted on Norwegian television or radio and that, too, is the subject of much heated debate nationwide, since the viewer's license fee goes up regularly, and in 1982 there were only 6.7 hours a day of transmission time.

In broadcasting one experiences more examples of the Norwegian penchant for being fair. In addition to programs in both official Norwegian languages and in Sami, there are at least short broadcasts in English wherever there are large numbers of English-speaking residents.

I've listened to panel discussion on the airwaves that could send the beginning language student into a serious case of shock. One person speaks Nynorsk, the next Bokmål, the third a dialect that combines both languages, while a fourth panelist may be a Dane or a Swede speaking that language and being answered in one of the varieties of Norwegian. The Dane, Swede and Norwegian treat each other as if they were speaking dialects of their respective languages.

Norwegians get into some of their more heated arguments about the benefits of Nynorsk over Bokmål (or vice versa) or the benefit of teaching dialect in the classroom. At the same time, however, they are genuinely surprised and flattered when an American or other foreigner is trying hard to learn the language. They have a bit of an inferiority complex about promoting their obscure North-European tongue (or two, or more), but they promote it endlessly anyway.

Semantic eye-openers

JOAN: Old Norse, dating from Viking times, supplied English with thousands of words. In more recent times the words that have made the transfer have been fewer. Ombudsman comes from the old Norse *umbodhsmadhr,* but only became popular after WWII. Quisling has become a universal synonym for traitor, and of course there are words like ski and slalom.

Unfortunately today the wave is going the other way. English is mixed with Norwegian without regard to good sense or style. American advertising methods have taken their toll.

But the semantics of a language tells a good deal about the psychology of the people. To say "I love you," using the exact words in Norwegian: "Jeg elsker deg," is almost impossible for Norwegians. One young woman said she could imagine saying it, maybe, just maybe, on her wedding day. To say the more general, casual, "Jeg er glad i deg," is much easier because it is unemotional, calmer, displays no passion.

It is to love in the sense of being fond, with no erotic overtones of any kind, no deep commitment.

Perhaps the most revealing difference found when Norwegian is compared to English is in the use of "please" and "thank you." There is no word for "please" in Norwegian. The closest that comes to it is the very rarely used, and extremely polite, "be so kind." One says, instead, "pass the salt, thanks."

Go into a store and listen. The salesperson says "Vær så god," which in this case really means "I'm paying attention to you." The customer, when paying, says "thank you" for the privilege of spending money. The salesperson only rarely says "thank you" for the sale. This is all relevant to the basic refusal to be subservient.

On the other hand it is obligatory, and forever retroactive and binding, to say "takk for sist" (thank you for the last time we were together). It doesn't matter if it's been ten years since you saw someone and were entertained in their home – you say "takk for sist". Equally obligatory is the statement "takk for maten" (thank you for the food). This is said when getting up from the table even if you're all eating in a cafeteria.

Make no mistake, there are just as many intricate forms of politeness in Norwegian – but none of them are subservient. A soldier salutes his superior officer and says "yes, Major." He never says "yes, Sir." There's no word for "sir" in the language.

Humor?

JOAN: Norwegians tend to put themselves down and say they are a humorless nation. Therein lies a great deal of their humor. They are filled with irony and sarcasm – directed at themselves. (But be warned, living in Norway does not give the non-Norwegian the right to put Norway or Norwegians down – they bristle and turn downright hostile if we're critical.)

The favorite brand of Norwegian humor can be detected through the homegrown fairy tales. Trolls are ugly, magical, often very wicked. They can be giants or they can be small, but the best thing about them is that they can always be tricked, teased or defeated by a clever Norwegian. There isn't as much light, teasing banter among Norwegians as among other peoples. It isn't that they take themselves so seriously, but they are very much afraid the other person is taking himself seriously and might take offense. Throughout history fist fights have been applauded as a way to save face – so even today a person is cautious about poking fun at another.

What surprises a foreigner is that although the language question is discussed endlessly, there is never the slightest irony or humor in the subject. To the newcomer it would seem these would be perfect topics for jokes, but for Norwegians the subject is too serious to laugh at.

A meager diet and physical training has made Norwegians a fairly healthy and slim people.

The same American ambassador mentioned earlier poked fun at a nation of four million people with two official languages (Bokmål and Nynorsk, new Norwegian, which is really an older Norwegian) plus the official Sami language, and no less than 272 separate and distinct dialects. It appeared to him, and to many newcomers, that all this space, these isolated communities, the many dialects, would make the people extremely different from the far north to the far south.

Amazingly, such is not the case and this can be easily noted in the restaurants and hotels. Fish is prepared identically wherever you are in Norway. The same pastries are served everywhere on identical doilies. The meatballs have identical tasting gravies. It's all much as it must have been a hundred years ago.

Unusual home styles

JOAN: Walk along the sidewalk in Hammerfest, Tromsø, Trondheim, Bergen, Kristiansand – and look at the windows in private homes. The curtains are identical. The plants in the windows are in identical pots. The only variation will be one identifying the age of the housewife: white or copper pots with begonias or geraniums for the older generation and some "newer upstarts" in ceramic pots or baskets in the windows of the younger generation.

Look carefully at Norwegian homes. While at first glance they do not appear so far removed from simple white frame or ranch-style homes in other countries, closer examination reveals additional proof of the Norwegian need for the outdoors, for light.

Nobody pulls a curtain or drape. It shocks the foreign newcomer to be able to see into, through, a Norwegian room – winter or summer. Norwegians sacrifice privacy willingly in order to have the outdoors coming in the windows. But even on a dark winter night it doesn't occur to them to pull the curtains and close the room inside. Perhaps there are symbolic lace curtains, which claim the inside privacy without hiding anything.

Lined drapes, so common in the English-speaking world, do not seem to exist, and the kitchen windows don't have proper curtains at all. From Kirkenes to Lindesnes the kitchen windows are decked with a useless ruffle, about seven inches wide, bisecting the lower third of the glass. All the light must come into the room.

In the winter the obsession with light is even more obvious: in nine out of ten Norwegian windows there will be a small electric light of some sort. Inside the room there will be way too many tiny lamps, small lights on walls, none of them strong enough to read by, but only there to illuminate each and every dark corner, to be "cosy." It's as if the coming of electricity provided a luxury with which to light the dark, but not necessarily to work by.

Many modern ranch-style homes and the duplex row homes are constructed with the living room and kitchen on the second floor and

Bakklandet in Trondheim is one of the many old urban areas being protected today.

the bedrooms laundry rooms on the first or ground floor. The view from the second floor is better. They rationalize away the inconvenience of going up and down the stairs to answer the front door by reminding the puzzled foreigner of the high incidence of fires in Norway and how much safer it is to sleep by the front door.

Confusing values

JOAN: Norway has different values to those found in other countries, and it can confuse a foreigner. A Norwegian who lives in a spacious home, perhaps with original art on the walls, bought as an investment, will still eat a piece of whole wheat bread, spread with margarine, and topped with one piece of cheese for lunch. Food is an item to cut for economy's sake. When they travel Norwegians are gourmets. At home they eat simply and sparingly with almost no imagination. The traditional food, what was good enough for grandfather, is good enough today. Food is plain, unspiced, repetitive. Stews, soups, boiled dinners prevail – and spare the budget. While the Frenchman or American may sniff at the peasant food of the Norwegian, they cannot help but be impressed by the extraordinary good health and beautiful bodies this spartan diet produces.

The moral is obvious, if depressing.

The food habits are an important factor in their health. To the dismay of experts from other nations who insist on blaming carbohydrates and starches for all ills, the average Norwegian breakfast is slice after slice of bread (albeit usually whole grain breads) with very little on top but their famous brown cheese, or goat cheese, or a slice or two of the superior Norvegia or Jarlsberg cheeses. Lunch is more of the same. Middag, or dinner, usually served right after work, simply isn't really dinner without potatoes – and boiled potatoes 90% of the time.

Bread

ARVID: Nothing so disappoints a Norwegian as traveling out into the world and discovering there is no place, not even in Sweden, to find Norwegian bread. When he arrives in the USA he finds the bread tastes like fog on an unusually sad day on the Newfoundland coast. That extra fine flour they use to make bread isn't fit to be eaten by him, or her.

It's doubtful if this whole grain bread is a hangover from the days when our ancestors, during bad years, had to mix the flour with bark from the alder, ash or willow. It's more believable that Norwegians are used to bread that tastes good, exciting, and they feel that it ought to be something worth chewing on. Statistics show that every fourth Norwegian family bakes its own bread and that more and more family men are doing the baking.

Today's Norwegian puts the bread which can't be used that day into the freezer and takes it out almost as fresh as new. Obviously they didn't do that a hundred or four hundred years ago. They baked "flatbrød," using a wafer-thin dough made from barley and oats which was baked over low heat. This made it crisp and evaporated all water. This way the bread could be stored for weeks, months and years.

Potatoes, always potatoes

JOAN: The four-year-old was suspicious of the soup the first day at nursery school and refused to eat. When coaxed he plucked out a white square and asked accusingly, "What is it?"

"Potato," said teacher.

"Oh, good, dinner," said the child and fell to.

A meal without potatoes is a snack, my Norwegian friend explained, adding, "After all, you can't mash rice or noodles into gravy and make do when there's no meat."

You'd think they'd invented potatoes instead of trying them for the first time in the 18th century. Are the people at the dinner table strangers, with nothing to chat about? No problem. They talk about potatoes.

Only Kerr's Pink potatoes are right for kumle, they told me. Kumle, or kumpe, or raspeballer, are heavy potato dumplings made with slight variations in ingredients and name from area to area. They are served with butter, salt lamb, mashed kohlrabi, and – you guessed it – more boiled potatoes.

But make no mistake, the potato to be boiled and served with the kumle must never be the one that was scraped to make the kumle. Heaven forbid. No. No. The potato to be boiled and served alongside the potato dumpling must be a Ringerike potato. (This is, of course, open to heated argument depending on where you come from.)

The long winter nights are cold and uninviting. Just right for cosy evenings at home.

And if you plan a fancy Sunday dinner with perhaps a roast leg of lamb: then it is obligatory to serve boiled potatoes by the name of Pimpernel – preferably grown on Jæren. (Can you guess that I've learned my Norwegian cooking on Jæren?) Don't forget the delicious potato pancake, called lumpe, which we wrap around a hot dog, or eat with butter and sugar; hasten to mention the lefse, another kind of potato pancake eaten like bread, or then again like a thin cake. For lunch there's potato soup.

As if all that wasn't enough, we can offer up a skoal to the potato – drinking the toast in the potato-based aquavit, of course. Linje Aquavit is as good as its journey over the equator is long. But brandy lovers should also try Brandy Special.

Norway has several good drinks. Norwegian Export Beer, on draft, is the world's best – and I am not listening to any dissenters. At just about 7% it is also a hearty drink. It's not on any label, so it helps to know that Pils has 4.5% alcohol, Brigg and Lettøl have 2.2% and Zero just that. The ads say that Lettøl has 26 fewer calories than skim milk.

Remember that Norway's drunk driving laws are very strict. One 2.2% beer an hour is about all a 150 lb. person dare drink and still drive a car.

Most towns have at least one "Vinmonopol," but small villages have none – and often even beer must be ordered by the case from the beer-selling grocer. You'll also be startled by the price: sins are taxed highly.

No gourmets here

JOAN: For all their world travels, the majority of Norwegians eat very simply at home. Meatballs and gravy will taste exactly the same whether purchased in a restaurant in Kristiansand on the south coast or in Tromsø in Northern Norway. In both places, too, rice porridge will

△ Outdoor grilling, over charcoal, is a brash new-comer to the Norwegian restaurant scene.

▽ Lefse can now be made on an electric skillet – instead of on a wood-burning stove. Whether they taste as good this way is open to discussion.

◁ If there are no potatoes on the table then it isn't a really proper, or good, dinner.

be the usual Saturday dinner – preferably with plenty of melting butter, sugar and cinnamon on top and accompanied by a glass of black- or red-currant juice.

Norwegians do not have any pretensions to being gourmets, although they love fine cuisine while in London, Paris or Rome. At home for the holidays they want boiled cod, boiled salt lamb ribs, a pork roast – of course with boiled potatoes.

Spices are coming slowly. Eight years ago it was hard to find fresh garlic in the stores but now even the "mama-papa" stores stock the breathless bulb. Fifteen years ago an elderly woman in Oslo tasted her first green olive and asked me, "What is this poisonous berry?" She'd never seen one before. Today olives and other exotic foods can be found in grocery stores all over the country.

ARVID: Gastronomy has never grown out of frugality. For hundreds of years Norwegians had to work hard to get the necessities to support life for themselves and their families. Ergo: in this country there's no food culture.

This assertion we have heard to the point of boredom from countrymen who have been on a week's package tour to the sunny coast of Spain, and now from foreigners who have been enticed here by our newly found riches.

"Ha! Norwegians eat boiled fish with boiled potatoes," maintain these people, with an indulgent tone that seems to shout that these are contemptible. I ask Our Lord to forgive them, for they do not know what they're talking about. And I propose, in the same breath and without casting my eyes down in shame: Norwegians have a culinary inheritance and tradition which few other peoples of the world can claim when it comes to distinction, variation, fine taste and delicacy.

All right, it isn't marked by fancy seasonings which only in the last decade have made their way to our northern reaches. But we've had our own, and above all: We have learned to prepare our food in a way that enhances the food's own taste qualities. Sure we're purists, and therefore we are a nation with a deep distrust of ketchup and barbecue spices which have invaded us from the American fast food industry.

So bound are we to our love of good food and drink that it had a central place in our Norse mythology. In "Håvamål," the song from on high, which any sensible person understands comes from the chief god Odin himself, one criterion is given for judging an insanity which is so pervasive that others have to take care of the crazy person. Odin says: "The person shall be declared incapable of managing his affairs who does not value food and beer."

JOAN: See what I meant about being careful how you criticize anything Norwegian?

Herring

ARVID: Herring, like flatbrød, is today, as always, a major staple on a Norwegian table, particularly on special occasions. The herring is prepared in all kinds of ways. Most widespread is the usual "sursild," herring in sour sauce. One takes "spekesild" (herring that has been sprinkled with sugar and salt and stored until it is mature), filetts it and cuts it up in bite size pieces. These are placed in jars or ceramic pots, layered with salt, sugar, whole white pepper, raw onion sliced wafer thin, whole cloves and bay leaf. When this is served, after standing for a day, it is unsurpassed as an appetizer. It is so good that you will simply want to stay at the herring table and continue with herring in dill, herring in sherry, herring in tomato sauce, herring in mustard, and more herring for as far as the imagination can stretch.

Cured, fermented and smoked

ARVID: Fish is fish, but meat is food, it's said some places. Not many Norwegians, and certainly not I, will agree. Fish has so many variations and taste-possibilities which meat doesn't have.

Going further along our Norwegian party table, we'll find salmon and trout – fresh, steamed, and set forth in full size; or smoked and sliced in gleaming, thin, slices. Trout will also be found "raket," fermented. This is a preparation method which demands the greatest cleanliness, where the fresh fish is cleaned and washed, rubbed well with salt, and laid lengthwise and tight down into tubs, under pressure, so air is kept out. After two or three months of storage at five to ten degrees Celsius it is mature, tender and easy to digest. As is true with good cheese, the smell of fermented fish can make the inexperienced turn their back. But the taste of fermented mountain trout is heavenly.

Jotunheimen – mountainous Norway at its most magnificent.

Flowers, as well as people, have had to get by on poor land, just like this poppy on Dovre.

"Grav," cured, fish, preferably salmon or mackeral, is easier to prepare. First the fresh fish is rubbed with a mixture of salt and sugar, then it is sprinkled with dill and laid in a cool place for a day or two.

Americans know that fish and shellfish caught off New England are much better tasting than those one gets in Florida. Among European chefs it is no secret that Norwegian fish products are preferred to those which are caught farther south. They also know that the simpler one keeps the preparation the better the taste will be.

Light makes taste

ARVID: Because of Norway's location, in the far North, with its hectic growing season having light almost around the clock, the taste of the berries, fruit and vegetables grown here is much more intense than in other places. Taste Norwegian strawberries, and you will know that you've never tasted strawberries before. Take something so prosaic as a Norwegian carrot and chew it raw. You will enjoy just about the same taste sensation noted when you get a good rare white wine.

Therefore there are many serious professional Norwegian chefs who lift a warning finger against those they maintain use too many seasonings. If, in spite of warnings, one wants some seasoning on a moose or reindeer steak, then some stirred fresh tyttebær (close to cranberries) or rowanberry jelly is as much as they will allow after perhaps a bit of salt and pepper.

Lutefisk

ARVID: We haven't yet spoken of the perhaps most peculiar of all Norwegian fish dishes. This is lutefisk, dried cod which is soaked and saturated with lye so the fish is soft and gelatinous when it has simmered a bit in boiling water.

Legend has it that lutefisk was discovered by a poor farmer in Gudbrandsdalen who, by accident, dropped some dried cod in a barrel of lye. He couldn't afford to throw away food, but also didn't dare eat it himself. Therefore he served it to his sick father since father was dying anyway. Then the wonder happened – father yelled for more, got well and was livelier than he'd been in many years . . .

Lutefisk is served with boiled potatoes, stewed peas and pork fat. If a Norwegian is invited to a good lutefisk dinner he'd go through tempest and fire to join in. For some strange reason not all foreigners are equally enthusiastic.

The story is told of the man in Minnesota who was plagued by a skunk under the stairs. He wrote to the advice column in the local paper for help.

"Put some food the skunk doesn't like under the steps. Try, for example, Norwegian lutefisk," ran the advice. Later, when they heard no more, the editor telephoned and asked how it had gone.

"Oh, yes, the skunk disappeared in a hurry. But now I have a new problem: What'll I do with all the Norwegians who are under the steps?"

Aqua vitae

ARVID: It must be admitted that one of the reasons for Norwegians being so fond of lutefisk and all the other specialties we have named is that the obligatory drink to have with it is ale and "akevitt," which is Norwegian for the Latin "aqua vitae," which means water of life and is a potato liquor.

Aquavit is a Scandinavian specialty. But of course there is a great deal of difference between that which is produced in Norway and that made in Denmark and Sweden. In our neighboring countries the raw alcohol is put right into the bottles. This makes the taste so acrid that it is suggested it be drunk ice cold. The Norwegian aquavit is made according to stringent regulations which mean it is stored in oak barrels for at least five years. In this way it has a well-rounded taste, and is as dark as whiskey. The Norwegian Linje Aquavit has an additional preparation which is unique: all the bottles with that label are taken on board a ship which is going to Australia and returning. On

the label it will say which ship it traveled on and the date.

The way this came about is as follows: back in the days when shipping wasn't as well organized as today, a captain took along some aquavit on a trip to Australia in the hopes of selling it at a profit. No sale was made and he had to take the bottles back to his starting point, Trondheim. There he discovered that a miracle had occured. On the long sea journey the liquor had completely changed character. The motion and the temperature changes had had such a positive effect that from that day it was a rule that bottles should be sent with each and every ship that went "down under." And pity the captain who tried to sell any of the load underway!

There are two reasons why Norwegian aquavit hasn't captured the world: because of the strict rules as to storing and maturing, the production is limited. In addition the national liquor monopoly has tried to sell its wares to a sophisticated market abroad while the Norwegian Storting has bound them hand and foot with a law that forbids advertising. The law against advertising doesn't just pertain to advertising for the home market, but has also forbidden advertising Norwegian liquor abroad. This is beginning to change.

I can't leave the subject of food and drink without saying something about Norwegian beer. Here too we have strict rules, fortunately, which means we are among the very few who still make beer of malt, hops and barley. All additives are banned, as is any grain other than barley.

Various Norwegian beers have several times been judged tops in American tests. One of the reasons for doing so well in competition can be said to be the Norwegian water which comes from undisturbed mountain districts where purity is high and the taste good.

So let's not tarry any longer, but rather say SKOAL, and you're welcome to come to the table.

The Protestant Church, whose prime goal was to make people audibly subject to the supreme King, did its best to suppress the Norwegian food culture right along with all the other national and rebellious characteristics. For example, psalms were written that said "In the sweat of your brow, shall you eat your bread."

Only in the most fundamentalist Christian areas was this taken so literally that people thought they ought to sweat when they ate. It firmed up the need to serve "bløtkaker" (a cake soaked in liquid) in all possible and impossible situations. In other places the heathen Odin and food culture have survived, although it is rare anyone drinks blood when good people gather to feast.

Pantheism?

ARVID: One wet and foggy late summer evening, while on a walking trip over Hardangervidda, I came down to a farm in upper Telemark. An old bachelor lived there who welcomed a lonely wanderer into his home.

△ Whaling used to be an important industry in Norway. This is the ship «Nancy Grey». The finback whale is today protected.

◁ A horned owl, after it has been registered and marked.

As we ate, and I must admit he served an unusually good homemade beer, he asked me where I was going. I told him, and he said, surprised, with a sparkle in his eyes:

"You have to be careful, I've heard they've become Christians down there!"

Contrast: In a small town on the south-west coast a new, liberal minister told a teetotalling fanatic that "You have to remember that Jesus turned water to wine."

"Ja," he replied. "We know it, but we don't like it."

The pietistic Christians in Norway were a deciding factor during the popular vote over the Common Market in 1972, when they practically unanimously said "no" out of fear that the Pope, and the Catholic Church, would get stronger.

Statistics are always an effective shield when one wants to lie, and the figures reporting church attendance say nothing about the people's religious life. Historically there has always been a conflict between the high and low church in Norway, between the clerical hierarchy and the layman in the prayer house.

This conflict also reflects the conflict between city and country, between interpreting the scriptures and believing in them literally. Visitors to Stavanger and other traditional centers for pietistic Christianity will insist there are entire streets lined with prayer houses, which is correct, but those who go there have their roots in the old country-style Christianity.

At its best this takes their roots back to Hans Nielsen Hauge, revival preacher and educator from the beginning of the last century, who many consider the one who actually brought Christianity to Norway, instead of the hero king St. Olav from around the year 1000, or Martin Luther.

My theory is that most Norwegians are nature lovers, and that those who have a background which blends State and Church as it was taught in school, carry with them a mental ballast which allows them to see the godly in nature. Most Norwegians prefer the creations of nature to the man-made churches, and they experience a mentally positive and valuable lift when they choose outdoor activities over a weekend instead of a passive seat in church. Therefore Norwegians are Pantheists.

JOAN: Arvid's right. Norway's religion is Pantheism. Jæren, the area on the south-west coast where I live, is viewed as Norway's "Bible belt." The people have the reputation of being pietistic.

Only a few days after I arrived here I was told that I must never, no never, hang out the wash, mow the lawn, wash the car or do any other outdoor work before 1 p.m. on Sunday. God forbid.

The church bells ring at 10 a.m. and 11 a.m. and chime through the

Bøya glacier, an arm of Jostedals Glacier.

peaceful countryside. But there is no rush to church. For the most part the people are all taking it easy indoors, until 1 p.m. The only thing to see on TV is a church service, with the exception of sport which seems to be exempt from the label of sin. And best of all – the telephone never rings before 1 p.m. on a Sunday.

Confirmation Sunday in May, when the year's crop of 13- and 14-year-olds fill the churches, reminds me more of a party than a spiritual solemnity. It is also possible that this is the only Sunday in the year when the parents go to church.

Confirmation for members of the Norwegian State Church also reminds me more of a Jewish Bar Mitzvah than a confirmation as it is practiced in other countries. It is a coming-of-age-ritual which only accidentally has a religious name. Part of the reason for continuing this connection between the Church and the teenage ritual has been the fact that the church minister used to be the official registrar. There was a time when a person who was not registered as having been baptised and confirmed could not get married, be eligible for some jobs, or get a passport.

Today everyone gets a social security number at birth. (It's slightly disconcerting to discover that the six first numbers are a person's birthday, which makes it impossible to lie about one's age.) The State does the registering now, but the tradition of confirmation is so strong that thousands of youngsters have a citizen's confirmation, a sort of non-religious substitute for this coming-of-age ceremony, an excuse to have a party and get presents.

Sun worshippers

JOAN: The long Easter holiday makes it sound as if the Norwegian is religious. The truth is that the holidays are observed in a fashion which helps solidify the belief that the people are sun worshippers. Norwegians often droop and complain of being "weather sick" during the darkest days from November to January. As the sunlight returns, the return of good spirits is also visible, and by Easter the population is bursting to get out on the mountain slopes with skis.

Perhaps Norwegians are not "born with skis on" as rumor has it, but their collective compulsion to disappear into primitive wilderness areas and welcome a snow-reflected sunburn seems like its own peculiar form of madness to a newcomer.

Everything stops at Easter. Even garbage collection is suspended for a week, on the safe assumption that no one is around to make it necessary. Besides, garbage collectors have a right to a holiday, too.

(One of the more astute observations made by an American visitor

Kirkehamn – church harbor – on the island of Hidra, just off Flekkefjord, where as late as in 1980 almost half of the working men were employed as fishermen. In that year the population was reduced to under 200, and the town was no longer considered large enough to be a town.

when asked what one thing impressed him most about Norway was: "It must be the only country in the world where all the garbage trucks are made by Mercedes!")

But of course church services do go on as usual. They simply do not have the large crowds that Easter brings out in other Christian countries. Polls show that only 49 percent of the Norwegians go to church even once a year. Yet it is typical that two of the other official national holidays are religious days which happen to fall in early summer.

Sporting life

JOAN: There are 10,452 sports associations in the nation, serving some 28 percent, or more than one million people. Forty-six varieties of enthusiasm are presented by individual organizations with probably the most popular being the Norwegian soccer association. Sports receive a good deal of financial support from the central government and the municipalities. The clubs and organizations also receive 50 percent of the profits from the enormously popular national soccer betting pools. The number of sports associations and clubs is quite astonishing when one realizes that most Norwegians are intensely personal, individual, about their athletic activities. This individual faith in the benefits of a healthy body can be seen by just looking around: people walk, they ride bicycles, they hike, they ski cross-country and they jog in ever greater numbers. Foreigners living here tell with awe of the "little old lady/man, of at least 85, who passed me by on a bike (or on foot, or on the ski trail, etc.)."

Each village has at least one soccer field, a gymnasium and usually a swimming pool. Tennis and squash halls are being built rapidly., The number of indoor swimming pools, for instance, is astonishing to newcomers. Marathon runs, orienteering, skiing of course, hiking in groups, are all increasingly popular. Whatever the question about mental or physical health may be, most Norwegians respond with "clean air, lots of it, and plenty of exercise."

Sporting spirit

JOAN: Again the government, local and national, does everything it can to promote such thinking with financial support. Norway's King Olav, at over 80, has been an avid sportsman and first in place at major sporting events. When the more than 600,000 Norwegians take to the ski slopes, they have at their disposal the world's longest network of prepared trails, marked weeks before with sticks and poles. The vacationer can travel from cabin to cabin, built and furnished by public funds, and pay a nominal sum for shelter and food (on an honor basis). The cabins are available summer and winter. Other "way stations" are hotel quality and help to subsidize the self-service cabins.

△ Norwegians are passionate sun worshippers. The mere glimps of the sun makes them stretch out on the strangest of surfaces in order to absorbe the lifegiving beams.

Year-around, there's room for all to feel at one, ▽ and alone, with all of nature.

The tourist associations do what they can to help ▽ the mountain hiker: blazing trails, supplying rope bridges.

Of course boating is a favorite sport and owning a small boat is taken for granted, it's as necessary for leisure activity as is the family cabin. This cabin, called a "hytte," must be built well away from civilization and be furnished in "old" style. This "old" furniture can be valuable antiques, the oil lamps may be supplemented with electricity and the outhouse may be replaced by running water – what is critical is the "atmosphere" of roughing it, of getting away from it all. It is not at all unusual to find a perfectly average family that has managed, often through inheritance, to own a cabin at the ocean and one in the mountains.

To a foreigner all these things mentioned are obvious wealth: vacations, culture, freedom from insecurity caused by worry about disaster, the leisure for sports, homes, cabins, boats and cars. It is obvious that anyone who owned home and cabin before the advent of oil and the latest period of inflation has to be viewed as rich by other nationals. But it is also true that home and property come first for Norwegians and they sacrifice other luxuries, such as dinners out in restaurants and fancy clothes, to pay for them.

OUR NORWAY

JOAN: Norway is primarily a mountain range and 50% of the country is bedrock. A mere 2.8% of the land area is cultivated soil; 5% is lakes, 20% is productive forest; and less than 1% is populated. All the rest is mountains or other unproductive ground. While it is true that Norway has the second lowest population density of any country in Europe, and is the fifth largest country in terms of area, the areas left unpopulated are empty primarily because they are uninhabitable.

From the farthest North, way above the Arctic Circle, to the tip of the southern coast –just a ferry ride away from the rest of Europe – this is one nation, with many similarities along its entire length. Yet dancing in rhythm with the similarities are the unbelievable and intriguing differences.

In the fog and the rain and the snow this is a land of dark magic and trolls. In the sunlight, the sparkle, the softness of berry time, this land is ebullient, laughing, celebrating life. I've come to sympathize with the "reserve" which is often a term used to criticize the Norwegian. If the inhabitants of this land allowed themselves to fall victim to the swings and contrasts of their surroundings they might, indeed, lose control of their senses.

Outdoor paradise

ARVID: Norway's four million inhabitants have a total living area of 323,878 sq. kilometers (125,050 sq. miles) to cling to. That is just about a square kilometer per person. Sometimes you get the impression that Norwegians are trying to utilize the entire land. Flying low over Norway on a sunny Sunday in March you can get the feeling, many places, that the entire population is out skiing. On paths and car-less roads in the woods around Oslo you'll meet more people on skis than you meet downtown in Oslo on an ordinary day.

If you like standing in line you can choose to go to one of the popular cabins where they serve fresh waffles and black-currant toddies. But if you prefer being entirely alone, you can choose an out-of-the-way track or make your own and not meet another soul except for a dancing hare in his white winter coat, a fox sporting a white-tipped tail, or the king of the forest, the moose.

The bear, wolf, lynx, and wolverine, which once were prevalent over the entire nation, have until just recently been in danger of extinction.

After being declared endangered species, and thus protected, the numbers have gone up slightly. The polar bear is not to be found on Norway proper, but lives in reasonably large numbers on Svalbard and Jan Mayen.

The battle by international environmental groups against whaling and sealing is not particularly popular. The hunters of these species feel it is no longer possible to earn a living. During these last few years

Visdalen in Jotunheimen

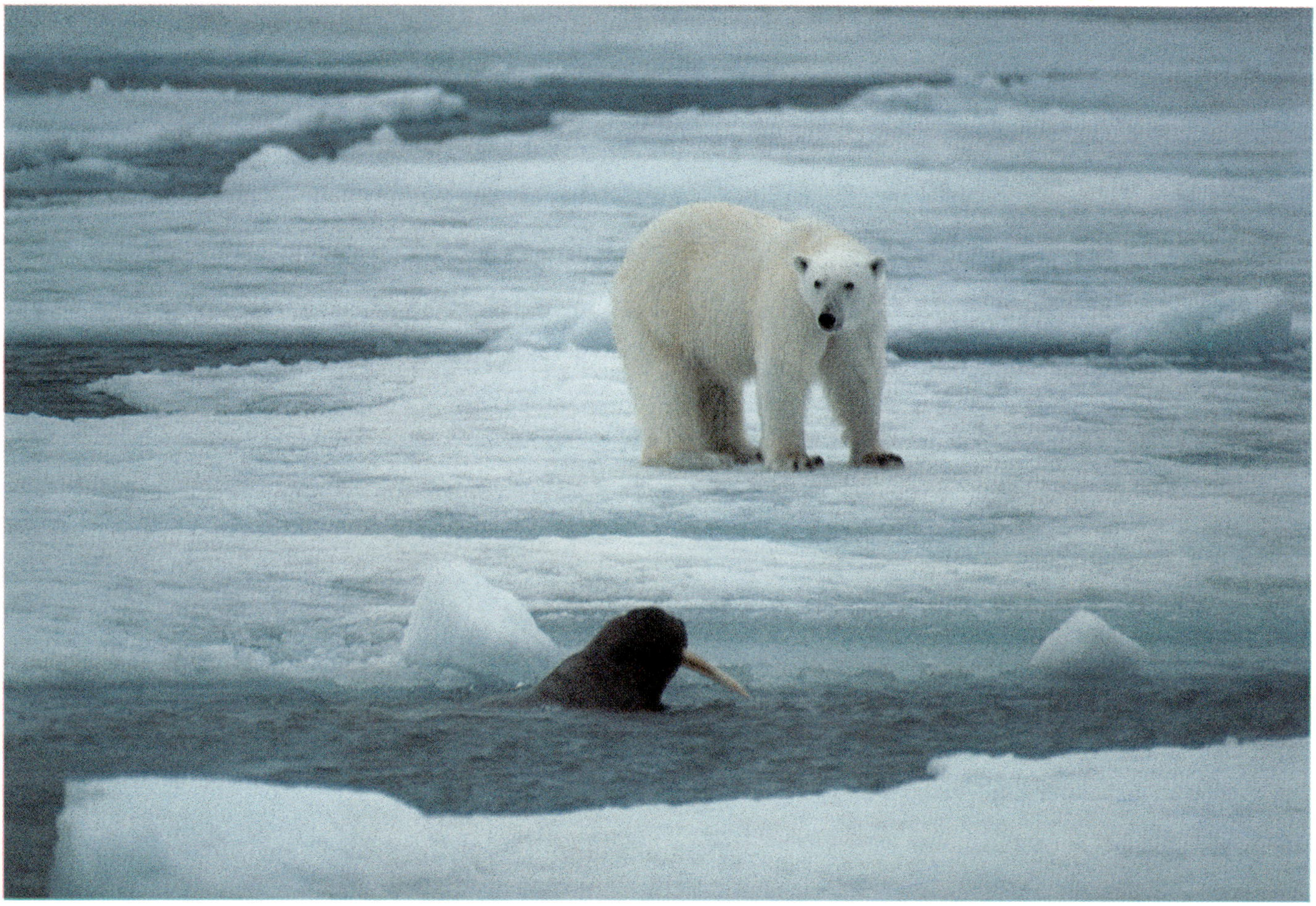

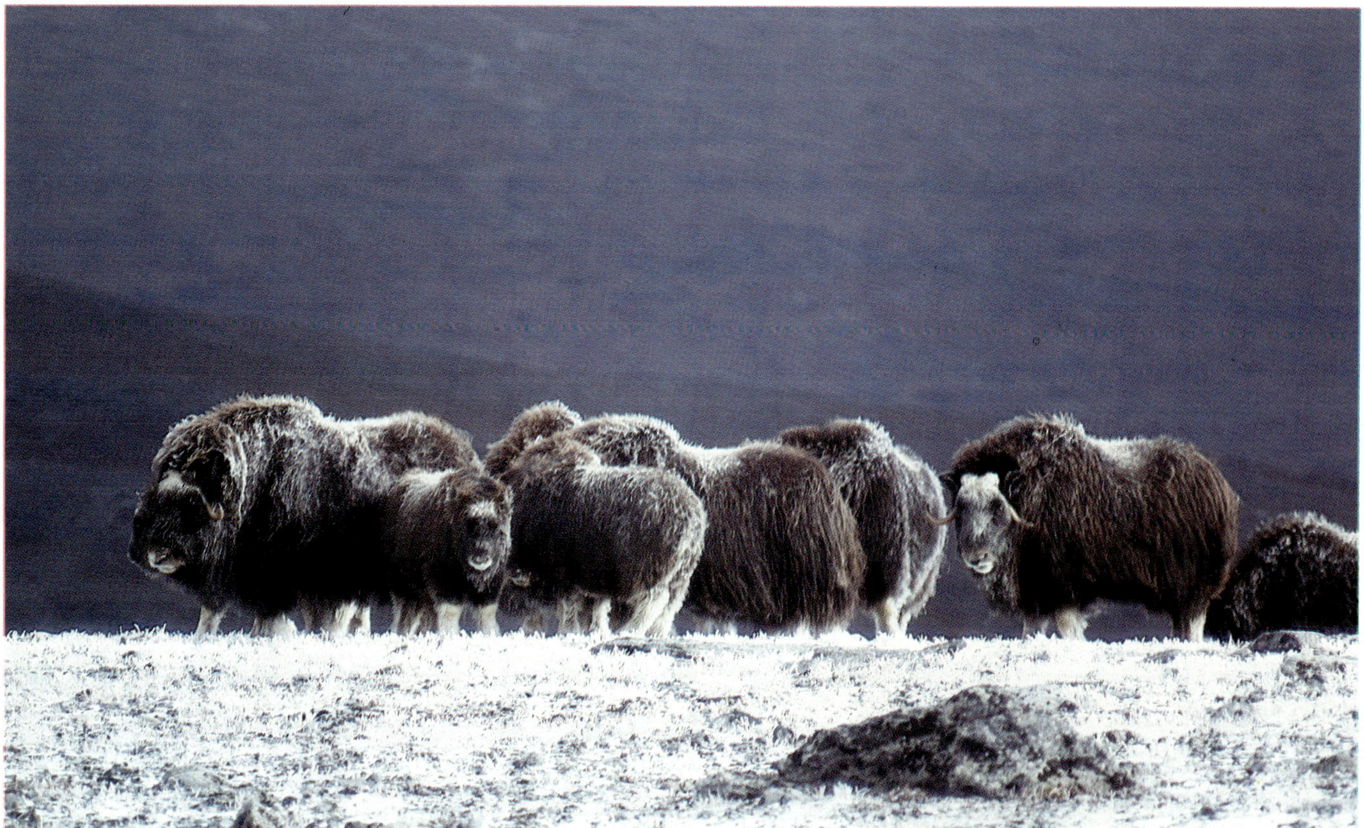

The polar bear calls Svalbard home. Once an endangered species, its numbers are increasing.

when the seal has been protected, there has been an explosive growth in their numbers; there are large colonies of seals as far south as the Oslo fjord. Fishermen, both those who fish professionally and those who fish as a hobby, complain that when seals are around the fish disappear and that seals ruin fishing equipment.

JOAN: That the Norwegians, in the face of worldwide disapproval, continue to indulge in whaling, makes no sense to foreigners – and puzzles a good many Norwegians. The whaling industry supports only a few people, and when boycotts are imposed on Norwegian products it actually costs more in lost revenue than it brings in. But even those fish-canning industries which stand to lose the most from boycotts are strangely silent as to the issue in general. They simply refuse to be quoted when journalists call.

200,000 lakes

ARVID: Norway is an eldorado for fishermen of all types. The possibilities for ocean fishing are limitless along the entire coastline, year-round but if you want to join the biggest of all ocean fishing adventures go to Lofoten and join the cod fishers in February and March. In addition there's good fishing in most of the 200,000 lakes spread over the entire country. There are also thousands of rivers and streams, with 200 of these registered as salmon fishing rivers. It is relatively expensive to fish for salmon, but for a minimal fee one can fish in all other places, right alongside the 200,000 registered Norwegian hobby fishermen. Among the salmon rivers the Tana in Finnmark is a star. During one summer season 50,000 kilo of salmon were caught with fishing poles.

In love with Oslo

ARVID: Compared with its more modern and sophisticated sisters, Stockholm and Copenhagen, Oslo is an "innocent country virgin," which is a quote from the snob magazine "Gentleman Quarterly" a while ago.

The picture isn't crazy. In addition Oslo is a good city to live in because it has cultural opportunities that equal or surpass those usually found only in much larger cities around the world, and because it is a paradise winter and summer for those who love outdoor life.

In area Oslo is one of the largest cities on the globe, but this is because the city owns large forests on its eastern, northern and western edges. The populated area is relatively small. All shops, museums, parliament-building, government offices, city hall and other important places are largely within walking distance from the main street, Karl Johan.

The hare and the owl are both night animals.

The musk ox, at one time also an endangered species, now ranges in the Dovre mountains.

Walking is the best way for tourists to get around in Oslo. It is the

fastest and easiest way to see the city center. Oslo's natives long ago gave up driving, because some authority or another is always digging up something and there's no apparent system as to which streets are one-way. Additionally those one-way streets can be changed from one day to the next without any warning. But if you're still dumb enough to choose driving, you'll discover there's no place to park.

Despite these things residents and tourists thrive in this city. During the sunlit summer Karl Johan and the student areas are outdoor roofless living rooms, with musicians and street peddlers and open air restaurants and lightly-clad people who seem to have all the time in the world.

In the winter there are glass roofs and walls on outdoor restaurants and the guests wear a few more clothes. Of course one has to go indoors to get a warm experience and that's not difficult. Take a walk down to Vika, five minutes from Karl Johan, to the new Concert Hall and experience the Oslo Philharmonic Orchestra which, under Mariss Jansons's direction, has become internationally known both on recordings and in concert. Or walk five minutes from Karl Johan in the other direction to the Norwegian Opera where singers, musicians and dancers present one success after another.

Det Norske Teater has recently moved into a palace of a theater complex, while the National Theater re-opened in 1985 after several years of restoration and rebuilding. In addition there are four other theaters and revue stages and a number of unaffiliated theater and ballet groups.

Oslo has a surprisingly large number of cafes and clubs where every variety of jazz is played, by local and visiting artists. Norwegian jazz has become world famous in recent years thanks to names like Jan Garbarek, Karin Krog, Laila Dalseth, Terje Rypdal and others.

Oslo is deadest on a Sunday morning in the winter. That's when "all" citizens are out skiing. Many residents live where they can put on their skis right outside their front door, others get to the countryside via car or streetcar. It is preferable to take the streetcar because then you can choose your route freely without worrying about finding your way back to your starting point.

There is no sport or open-air activity which can't be practiced within the city's borders, summer or winter. You can sail or swim in salt water, or in fresh water if you prefer it. You can go ice skating or slalom skiing. You can borrow a bike and take a long ride out in nature where you won't see or hear a car. It's possible to see a fox or moose, or a hare, within Oslo's borders.

I am a newcomer to Oslo, but have fallen so in love with this city that I can't imagine why anyone would have the heart to leave it. At least, never in the summer.

Oslo's City Hall shows in the background.

An idyllic scene from a
picture postcard – but
everyday living to the
people of Akerøy harbor,
just southeast of Lillesand.
What makes it so photo-
genic is the pride shown
in restoring and maintain-
ing old homes.

Each small town along the
southern coast seems
more pristine, pure, then
the next.

JOAN: Driving south along the coast from Oslo, it is possible to put the car onboard one of the world's smallest ferries, big enough for only two cars and a bicycle. A handful of passengers watch as the tiny boat maneuvers the narrows from route 351 at Øysang across Nordfjorden to the landing in the very center, the heart of Risør.

If only there weren't any automobiles. Without the discordant note of modern machinery the journeyer would believe she'd stepped through time to re-enter the 18th century. The small wooden homes with varicolored slate or tile roofs look as they must have 150 years ago when fishermen came home after a long day out on the Skagerrak.

But don't be deceived into believing these very old white frame homes, or others in towns all over the country, are a sign of poverty. The Inspectorate of Historic Buildings has decreed that heritage must be preserved and I have personally watched as an old, charming, wooden home was taken apart board by board and transformed – inside only– into the most modern of dwelling places, to which the ancient boards were then carefully re-applied, one by one.

Vacation weather

JOAN: In the many coves at Risør the water of the Skagerrak is almost tropical in summer, the rocks hot in the sun, the frolicking naked babies brown and their hair bleached white. The air is soft and languorous, the land abundantly rich.

Further south along the coast lies Arendal, once called Norway's Venice because the town was built upon seven islands. Inevitably progress meant filling in the areas between most of these and Arendal is no longer a city of canals but a modern seaport with an excellent and protected harbor.

Arendal, a prime tourist attraction in the summer, is often full of English visitors, and a bit further along the coast one finds Lyngdal jam-packed with Germans. Tromøya, one of Arendal's many islands, is a popular camping-ground.

It is in this part of the country where all Norwegians who prefer ocean to mountain want to have a cottage. The beaches are clean, the sides of the fjord aren't too steep, and the water is clear and almost completely unpolluted. What keeps these beaches from being overcrowded is that the temperature is about five degrees below what a person would call warm. The fastest growing activity along the southern coast is windsurfing, and with a wet- or dry-suit nobody has to worry if the water is a bit cold.

If you are lucky enough to be driving this way be sure to take a detour from E18 and go through the small towns which the main road bypasses: Grimstad, Lillesand, Mandal – the one more charming than the next. If you'd like to live as the Norwegian vacationers do, try spending the night in a "husrom til leie," which is the same as a tourist home in the USA or "bed and breakfast" in Great Britain. But check whether breakfast is included.

To rent a "hytte" means you'll be in a dollhouse-sized cabin with bunk beds, table, hotplate, service for four and sometimes a refrigerator. You bring linens and everything else. The bathrooms and water are in a common building. You could also try a "rorbu," which is the name of a tiny house hanging over the sea where the fishermen used to stay when they came on shore.

My personal favorite among all the overnight possibilities is a "føderådstue." This is the farm's oldest home, left standing after the new one was built, so the old folks would have a place to live when junior took over the main house. Pensjonat, gjestgiveri and fjellstue are the names of small hotels with prices that are kind to the budget.

If you're hunting for a place to eat in a village, don't be afraid to try the cafe or restaurant at the railroad or bus station. They are clean and serve ordinary home-cooking.

The southern coast has winter weather much more severe and long-lasting than those areas further north but on the western coast. When Stavanger, for example, is decked out in bright raingear in March, Arendal will still be digging out from under snow drifts – all because of the whims of the winds and the gifts of the Gulf Stream. All this changes in the summer and Arendal and the coast all the way down to Lindesnes, Norway's southernmost point, can often become downright hot.

If everyone's most pagan prayers are answered, and Midsummer Night is sunny and warm, this southern coast takes on the air of sensuous sun-worshipping indulgence. Everyone who can make any excuse to do so is at the water's edge or in a boat, literally lolling, watching over bonfires sacrificed to the gods of the light.

Along every small dirt side road on this coast can be seen tourist campers and, just over there, a tiny delicate roe deer, ears alert, one foot raised and poised for flight, stares quizzically at the tourists, who in turn stare back and sigh. Wilderness and its animal life co-exist in a fine balance with the encroaching humans – in much the same way as they have done for a thousand years.

Here and there, too, can be seen large and obviously artificial mounds which the natives will say are burial mounds of Viking kings or queens. One of these is to be found outside Vigeland, on E18.

My own personal summer idyll is Lyngdal. There are two fine beaches here. The one, Rosfjorden, is usually overcrowded with German, Danish and Norwegian campers. But the other, Lyngdalsfjorden at Kvåvik, is almost always empty and it slopes so gently and carefully into the sea that it is an ideal playground for small children. The water is shallow for such a long distance that it is also often pleasantly sun-warmed. Or drive north along the Lyngdal River and you will find swimming "holes" filled with summer-bronzed children.

In between the rocks animals and grass thrive. Jæren is wild, untamed, and yet abundantly rich in its gifts.

Jæren's Rev is treacherous. Yesterday this was a safe and secure small-boat harbor.

North of Lyngdal, at Vemestad, there is a sheer rock wall stretching up hundreds of meters into the sky, hidden in the wood and greenery. On the face of that perpendicular wall is an exact cut that is clearly a Christian cross. You see, there was once a cave there, and inside lived a whole family of fierce and terrible trolls that terrorized the whole valley with their mischief. But one day the holy St. Olav came riding through the valley with his men and the people in the valley beseeched him to do something about the trolls. With a mighty heave he threw his sword against the mountain, causing the cave to close over and the sword to dig deeply into the stone and leave the cut cross as the lock to bind the trolls. And here they will stay forever, locked in the rock and unable to escape, St. Olav promised, as long as the cross remains intact.

Follow the coastline and suddenly, so suddenly as to bewilder the senses, the landscape changes somewhere just before Flekkefjord. Here the gods have been playing games: a giant became angry one day and in a terrible temper began throwing the mountains into the sea. Everywhere boulders, whole hillsides, tumble, come rolling, cascade to the sea and it is a daring, twisted little tree that tenaciously clutches to a rock with its roots exposed. In spots here the landscape is as barren as the surface of some airless moon circling a far distant planet.

Stavanger is both a modern oil city and an old romantic town.

This is Jæren

JOAN: Where the coast of West Agder becomes Rogaland there are other radical changes in the landscape. The same giants who so capriciously tossed mountains at the sea seem to have stolen away all the trees in those days before humans made up their minds to disbelieve and thereby drove the giants into exile. Rogaland is windswept and rugged along its rough coastline.

Where the giants' boulders landed in the sea they became treacherous reefs that have claimed the lives of countless seafarers. Today's small-boat owner wanting to make the trip from Egersund to Stavanger joins the convoy set up regularly by the coast guard. Anyone growing up on this coast has heard the tales of gallant rescues by farmers with ropes; seen paintings depicting the hopelessness of the landbound as they stood and watched a fair and lovely sailing lady flounder on the rocks, the rocks called "Jærens rev." Every year the underwater demon the sailors call "Rasmus" claims its share of the lives that would dare to trespass on its domain. No matter how modern the equipment – when the waves are stirred to a ferocious boil and the wind that Rasmus blows is in power – the sea demon takes its toll.

Strangely the land on this southwesternmost curve of the country is flat, or flat when compared to the rest of the coastline. There are verdant fields with grazing cows so full of milk they often need brassieres. Only look again at the fields. See the stone fences. Imagine

the price levied for claiming this land from the boulders and rocks in the days before there were mechanized lifting machines. Imagine the generations of men wielding levers to lift, and then laboriously drag, the boulders along the earth to the boundary line. Jæren was once the poorest part of Norway. When the gods decreed that the herring desert the waters off this coast, the fishing industry that had been the backbone of the entire area wasted away. Despite the rain, and the early Spring that allows the farmer at least two crops a year, Jæren was poor and getting poorer. Then oil was found under the ocean that had once provided herring. Now this part of Norway is the nation's richest.

History everywhere

JOAN: In the year 872 Harald Fair Hair fought a ferocious battle in the fjord that lies between Sola and Stavanger. He won the battle of Hafrsfjord and Norway was united at last under one ruler. All around the area can be seen stone monuments to him and to Erling Skjalgsson, from Sola, who freed his slaves a thousand years before this became a popular philosophy.

All along this coastline, too, can be found archeological treasures that date man's occupation here back to the beginnings of the current climatic period. Traces of Stone Age and Iron Age man join scattered Viking remains, proving that Norway has always been "the way north."

This part of Norway has the mildest climate, fewer extremes, than any other. There are only a handful of days on the coast at Stavanger with snow or ice, and an equal handful of days with truly warm weather. The nearby mountains of Ryfylke will be still topped in white snow as the farmers on the coast are talking spring. This is sheep country and Spring is measured in lambs. When the lambs are to be seen outdoors it's summer, no matter the rain. Because it does rain. In some years it rains so incessantly as to wipe the smile off everyone's face.

Rainbow country

JOAN: But there is a rainbow outside my window at least twice during every rain. It is the cleansing rain that makes the air so sweet, the countryside so green and lush. This, out of all the various areas of the country, is where I choose to live. Jæren is my home and I am fiercely prejudiced in its favor.

Jæren's moods

JOAN: Lost in swirling mist I feel poised on the edge of the world. There is no reality but my body: no east or west, right or left. The world is lost and only I am found.

The rocks of Jæren. There will be as many rocks that have long since sunk beneath the earth as can be seen above it.

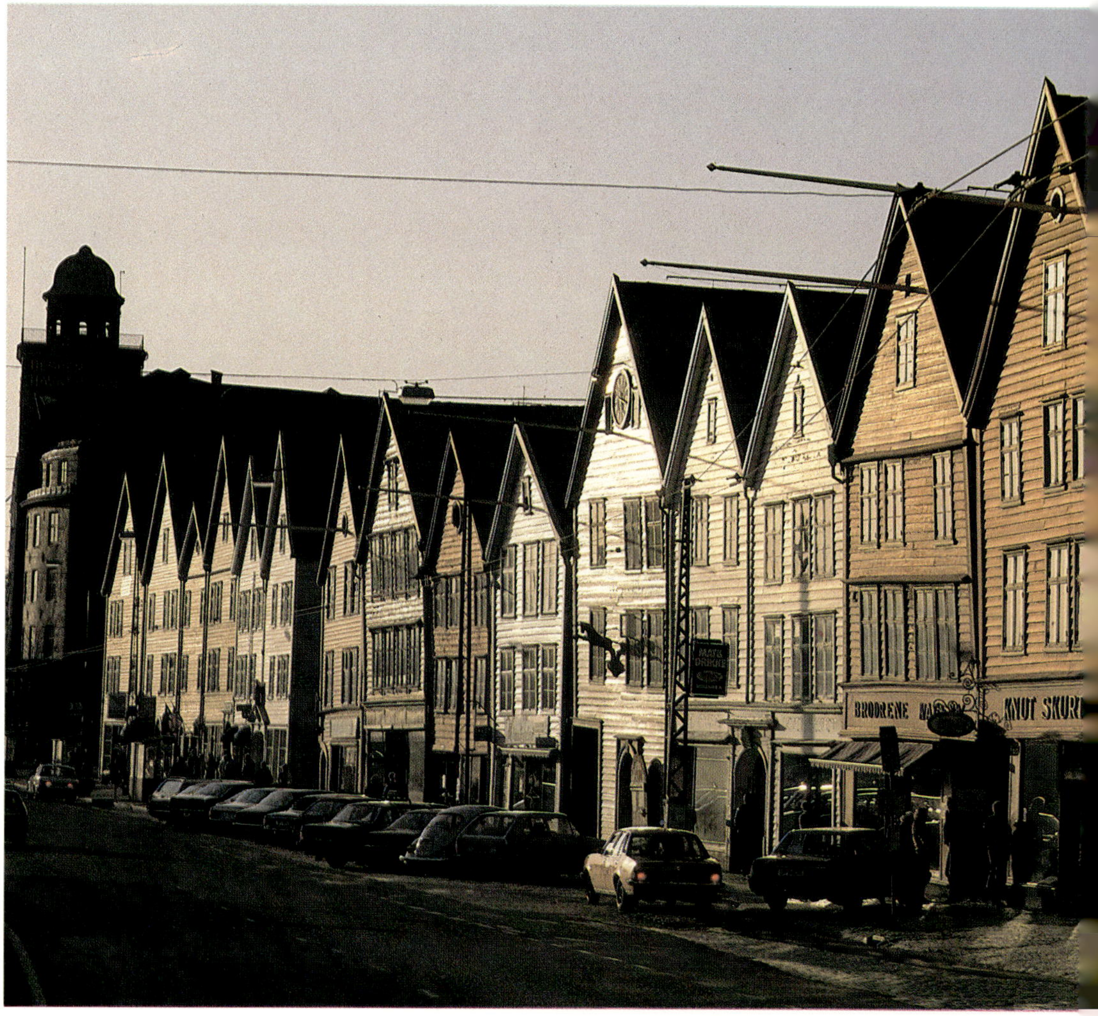
BRODRENE

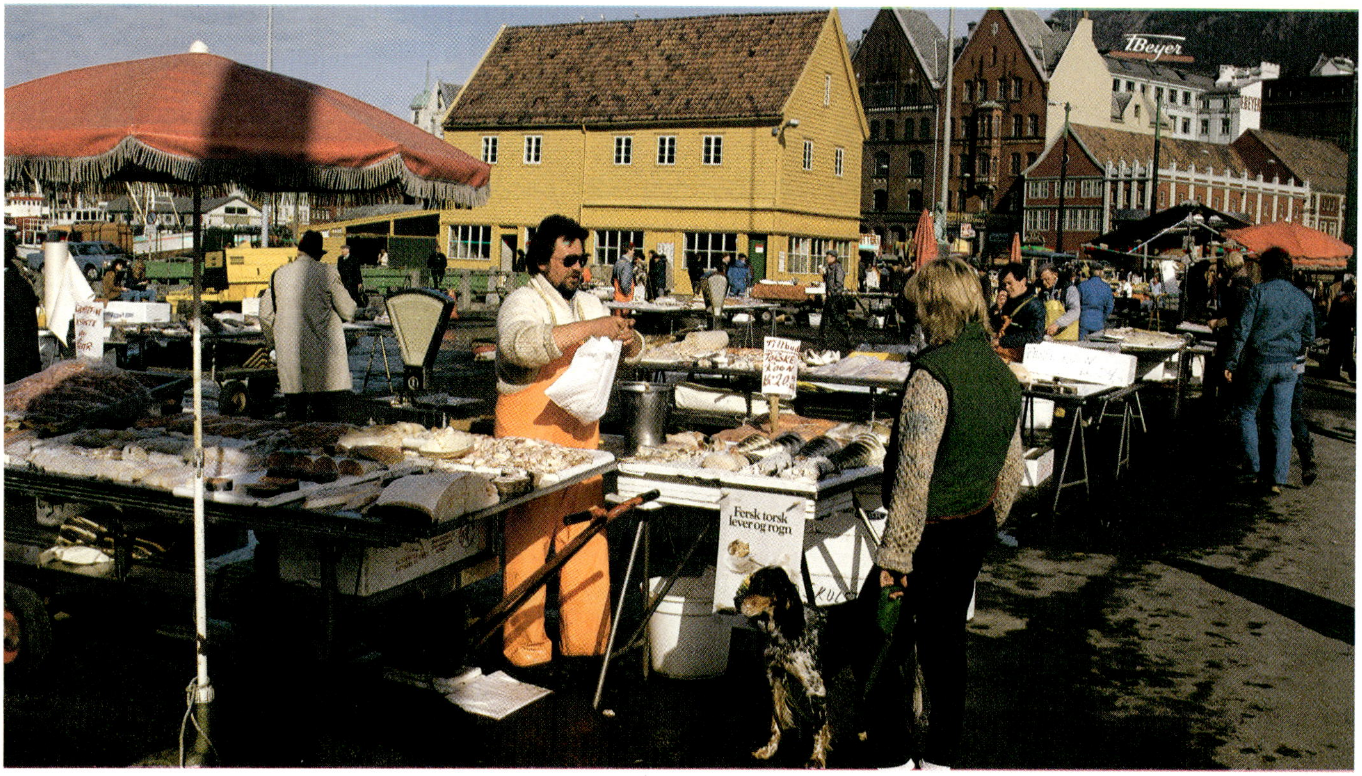
Fersk torsk
lever og rogn

△ Bergen is a friendly, cheerful, city that has done a beautiful job of restoring its Hanseatic waterfront.

It rains in Bergen, so they say, and grumble. But ◁ the rain is also what makes the air so delightful, the colors so clear, the foliage so lush.

◁ Bergen's waterfront fish market, like those to be found everywhere along the coast, is a feast for the eyes and an appetite teaser.

Tantalizing tendrils of smoky fog weave a complex web of cool mist around me. The silence is so heavy that a sudden screech from a seagull makes me gasp. Must I weep along with the utter desolation of the fog horn, heard mourning sadly, gently through the thick wet? The sob of the fog horn adds power to the silence without really adding sound.

When I walked out onto the beach the fog was coming in, visibly, pulsatingly, rolling across the water: white and inexorable. I stood still watching until I, too, was lost within. And now I dare not move, for fear the movement would be in the wrong direction and I, too, will become one more forlorn captive of the eternal mist. Shrouded spiritually as well as physically I huddle, tugging at the wool sweater beneath the sturdy, modern slicker suit. They are real. My hands turning red are real.

Time, as measured by clocks, even life, seems to flow out and away, as the sweetly seducing swirls whisper songs of trolls and fairies, elves and mermen, epic tales of Loki and Freya. Suddenly the slap of a wave sounds ominous. The shadow – just there – is it a sea monster?

From behind comes the whisper of a wind, a light kiss of a breeze mixing with the wet, teasing the edge of my scarf. Clearly I am the only human alive anywhere: there is only the sea, the automated fog horn, the mist, the bird, and me.

Alone. So alone.

Now the breeze gathers strength and the grey, oppressive wet shroud begins to sway, to move. The sounds change and instead of the dirge made up of fog horn, bird, and sea slap, there is a faraway counterpoint of happier sighs.

Ponderously the fog lifts, the mist thins. White light shines behind the clouds. Above me appears a golden circle. It feels as if the very air will explode into creative life.

All the logical, scientific explanations escape my feeling mind. To my senses it appears that the dark spirits, the sprites of despair, have decided to play elsewhere, torment someone else with their tauntings of loneliness. At least for today.

With the sun's return comes the overwhelmingly luxuriant and succulent world, throbbingly alive. Green and white and yellow and grey rocks, blue sea, dancing white and gold light rays on water blind my still shadowed eyes. The very song of the bird changes from wail to joy. The sob of the fog horn? Why, it has gone. I can hear a ferry coming into the harbor, its whistle cheerfully bragging of another safe crossing.

This is Jæren. Jæren, where the sun's rays cast a strange, other-worldly, light. A light that is sometimes colored apricot and other times a blinding robin's egg blue. A light unlike that found anywhere else in the world. The light on Jæren is poetry. It is such a mystical and indefinable poetry that it can make an artist go mad with inadequacy.

* * *

JOAN: Stavanger is Jæren's, and Rogaland's, capital, and the city struggles with the conflict between being a quaint old-fashioned fishing village and a glass-and-steel towering oil center. With admirable perseverance the city planners hold on to the cobblestones, seaside warehouses, brightly painted small houses that twist and turn,

Probably the most photographed waterfall in a land of a million waterfalls is at Geiranger. This is where the cruise ships come in, to tourist gasps of wonder.

that way and then this, as they curtsy and bob at each other across narrow little lanes winding down the hillside to the sea. Other tensions, between old-fashioned puritanism and modern sophistication, between the austere life and the lavish, provoke those who call themselves "Siddis" (or citizens) into endlessly challenging dialogues.

On the way to fjord country

JOAN: By car and ferry it is only a morning's journey from this southwestern corner up into the fjord country of the travel brochures. Drive north along E76 and at the spot where route 47 goes further north and E76 contines back eastward, the journeyer has one of the unsolvable problems always cropping up: which way to go? Further along E76 there's the southern edge of the Hardangervidda and Roldal. In Roldal there's a magical stave church where the crucifix was said to sweat on Midsummer Eve, back in the days when faith was perhaps more a part of every worshipper's fabric. If the believer wiped a drop of the wooden Christ's sweat onto a linen handkerchief and then onto a wound, a blind eye, a twisted leg, a cure might result. In a museum in Bergen can be seen the discarded crutches, stretchers, etc. No one is willing to explain to me why the miraculous cures stopped when the Reformation came to Norway.

If, instead of the inland road, we choose to continue northward on route 47 the instant reward is Låtefossen (for the romantic this can be translated to musical falls). The double waterfall roars down with spray and incredible power all year, to delight the passing tourists in busses and cars. This is also the only spot I've found in Norway where a souvenir stand has been built to cater to the visitors, and built in such a position as to interfere with photographic efforts. One of the irresistible charms over most of Norway is that it hasn't been commercialized, exploited.

After Odda comes Sørfjorden, an arm of the famous Hardangerfjord. Driving the narrow route 47 the Folgefonn Glacier can be seen across the fjord on top of the precipitous peaks. Cherry and apple trees wave enticingly at passing humans, and small homes snuggle against the cliffs. Children sell strawberries, apples, cherries along the road in season.

At Ullensvang, just beside the constantly expanding modern tourist hotel, can be found the tiny wooden cabin where Edvard Grieg's piano is glimpsed through a window. His music on the car cassette player adds the musical counterpoint to what is being seen in Hardanger.

Come along now to discover my secret place. We take a ferry from Kinsarvik out into Utnefjorden and wait, with breath held, to arrive in the miniature idyll of a tiny town called Utne – and a stay at the Utne Hotel. This is Norway's oldest hotel, founded in 1725 as a coaching station.

The Utne Hotel is a place to go to hide, to lick the wounds our electronic age inflicts, to heal the battered senses. My spartan room has housed generations of travelers. The fruit tree outside my window taps love songs against the panes. Or perhaps I have a waterfront room with a pocket balcony and can sit and contemplate nothing more important than the coming and going of the faithful ferry.

There's no excitement in Utne, but the food served by the friendly hostess is excellent. There's no nightlife in Utne, but the nearby museum testifies to the tough fiber of the men and women who called this home. There's no amusement hall with electronic games, but there's coffee or tea, from a silver service, poured by the hostess for her guests in a room that can only be called a parlor, while her relative, the watchful Mother Utne, looks down at us from a painting on the wall.

Everywhere along this adventure going north the lure of the side road is a siren's song that no one should deny. Getting off the main road and down a dirt path is to discover the song of the bees and imagine conversations among elves, who, of course, are hiding in the blades of grass or behind a wildflower.

From the Utne Hotel the visitor can go on around the point westward to Norway's only barony, in Rosendal. Or do as we do each time we visit, take the ferry back to Kinsarvik and drive up to Vøringsfossen where there's a perpetual rainbow when the sun shines. Highway 7 also goes north and east over Hardangervidda and gives the motorist a complete impression of the tundra's wildnerness, where only reindeer feel at home – plus of course the hiking and skiing Norwegians.

From here north, along and around endless numbers of fjords, over ever higher mountains, the adventure Norway offers the curious and fascinated is as changeable as the winding road.

Unlimited delights

JOAN: Bergen, Ålesund, Andalsnes, Trondheim, Tromsø, all the way to Hammerfest, each city has as many mysteries uniquely its own as it has similarities such as fish markets or bright flowers in windows.

The photographer who at first stopped to capture each waterfall, quickly decides she will run out of film and money before the countryside runs out of new and more spectacular falls.

Ålesund was suddenly the center of attention in 1985 after the English TV series "Maelstrom." The fjord which ends abruptly at Geiranger is the most photographed in tourist brochures and on cruise ship posters. The problem with fjord country is trying to decide which one to explore first. Each new fjord is more fascinating than the last. But if you're in this area you might as well gather your courage for the climb up "Trollstigen" and after surviving the endless hairpin curves take a rest in the pleasant restaurant at the top. There you can regain your strength on delicious "rømmegrøt" (sour cream porridge) and buy a diploma to back your claim to the adventure.

In Loen, at the innermost edge of Nordfjorden, you can take a walk on Jostedal Glacier, and fish in icy, clear blue waters.

Ålesund, the stepping stone to all of the western coast.

Ona lighthouse shows the way into Romsdalen.

Anybody lucky enough to be in Trondheim at the end of July ought to take part in the celebration of the St. Olav Days in the magnificent Nidaros Cathedral. Be sure to take a look at the now dry well, which once upon a time was the source of miracles. Take the time, too, to drive 80 kilometers north to Stiklestad to see the St. Olav Pageant staged each summer in a beautiful outdoor amphitheater. In order to follow the action, stop at the information office first and get an abbreviated copy of the manuscript in your own language. I saw this pageant for the second time during a terrible downpour, but was so spellbound that I wasn't even tempted to seek shelter.

On the way to Stiklestad, or the way back, you have to stop off in Hell. It's only a railroad whistle stop, but most English speaking tourists get great delight out of having their passports stamped here, or in sending a postcard home saying, "You always said I'd end up here . . ."

From the sea, perhaps comfortably watching from the deck of the coastal steamer, the rocky fjords and isolated pocket communities look strangely disconnected, as if they were islands suspended in time and space. Driving through them, while attempting to breathe again after the last harrowing mountain pass, the same towns look like living trophies to the human courage and tenacity that has made them survive.

The mountain ranges become wilder, more rugged as one goes north and on top of a few there are Sami waiting to sell homemade moose- or reindeer sausage and bone souvenirs. In Tromsø the museum keeps alive and preserves the rapidly disappearing life of the Sami. In Hammerfest the happily gullible tourist can become a member of the "Royal and Ancient Society of the Polar Bear," founded in 1962!

Bewitched by Northern Norway

ARVID: Anyone who has truly experienced Northern Norway will have lost their heart to the scenic beauty and the people, who are so different from those in the rest of the country. For some strange reason there isn't the reserve and distance that marks the southern Norwegian. A foreigner here is met with a warmth and spontaneity which is more like that to be found in Mediterranean countries.

While I was in the military I went on leave and took a fishing trip to a mountain lake in Inner Troms. At 4 a.m. the Midnight Sun was high in the sky, as it had been all night, and I began to make my way back. After walking awhile I realized I was going the wrong way.

Shortly afterwards I came to a farm in a small valley. The farm dog began to bark and woke up the family. A window opened, and a tousled head popped out and asked who I was. I answered, and was told that I didn't have permission to go any further before I'd had a cup

Northern Norway, and particularly Lofoten, is the most magical part of this country.

of coffee. A short time later the whole family was sitting around a table laden with the best the house could offer. Never has a meal tasted better. Despite the inconvenience, the man of the house took out the truck and drove me back to camp.

Some years later I vacationed with my family on the small island of Hekkingen, far out in the Polar Sea off the coast at Tromsø. During the 14 days we were there we never wore more than shorts and bikinis. When we traveled south again, by coastal steamer, we sat on the top deck in the same outfits, without being cold.

If you trace the 69th latitude which goes through Tromsø west, you go through the middle of Greenland and Baffin Island and bisect the northern part of Alaska. Nevertheless one can experience a tropical summer, as we did, where the night temperature doesn't go below 20 degrees Celsius, and where the maximum temperature can go above 30 degrees Celsius. But to be fair, such a dream summer doesn't happen very often.

Tromsø has often been called Norway's Paris, and when it comes to restaurants and nightclubs there's no place in Norway with a greater number in comparison to the population. The last ten years Tromsø has become a University town and has acquired a regional theater. Cultural life is blooming. Here, as everywhere in Northern Norway, it seems that the verbal story-telling tradition has survived better than in other places and nowhere else can one get a story served up that is so juicy, but still so short and to the point.

JOAN: I was surprised over how many people talked to me on a first of May in Tromsø. They bubbled over with good humor and happiness because the sun was shining and insisted that I had to buy an ice cream cone because it was May 1. At least six people told me the exact day when the Midnight Sun would appear and the opposite date when the night would win over day.

JOAN: *This is Norway, too – my Norway and Arvid's Norway – a land of constantly changing contrasts and extremes. Always dramatic, always a feast for the senses, always fulfilling – but forever challenging and bruising the emotions, assaulting human frailties.*

Sometimes it is almost more than a human, a mere mortal, can endure: there are too many changes, too much beauty to take in without feeling engorged. In the winter the long dark takes away the will to live and work and it would be easy to hide in a cave and sleep, and sleep. In the summer the sunlight at night is enough to make dancing feet lose the way home and keep right on following any pathway to new and more delicious delights.

It only remains for each new visitor to find the magic spot with the special appeal that sparks his or her imagination to new heights.

Welcome to Norway.

Senja in Northern Norway

PHOTOS BY

A-FOTO: 22, 24, 42, 45, 68–69
   Rolf Øhman: 10
   Rolf M. Aagaard: 14
Andersen, Jørn A.: 55
Bang, Hans Hvide: 13, 37, 38, 63, 91
Berge, Johan: 19
Bratlie, Espen: 59
J. W. Cappelens Forlag A/S: 80
Eidstuen, Hans: 8
Eikerappen, Torhild: 97
Fjellanger Widerøe: 26
Flobak, Tormod: 76
Furuhatt, Ernst: 49
Garborg, Olav: 98
Gilbert, Mats: 57
Grastveit, Jostein: 35
Gundersen A/S, Alf: 33
Hart, Kim: 4, 11, 37, 50, 52–53, 54, 55, 62, 70, 74–75, 83, 87, 94–95
Haukeland, Per: 6
Hermansen, Pål: 2, 12, 20, 79, 88, 90, 111
Hov, Jon Østeng: 91
Jacobsen, Bjørn: 29, 35
Jonsson, Per: 99

Knudsens informasjon: 66
Langenes, Alf: 40–41, 79
Larsen, Thor: 90
Leren, Eiliv: 108
Melbye, Bjørn: 18, 23, 77
Mittet Foto A/S: 73
Norsk Data: 33
Rafaelsen, Ellinor: 62
Røe, Ola: 21, 30, 48–49
Samfoto/Trygve Bølstad: 22, 27, 32
   Svein Erik Dahl: 48, 51, 64
   Ola Lagarhus: 34
   Rune Lislerud: 10
   Per Anders Rosenkvist: 60
Skramstad, Trygve: 85
Solvang, Frits: 64
Statoil: 30
   Leif Berge: 31
Sunde, Helge: 11, 14, 16, 19, 24–25, 38, 46–47, 49, 50, 65, 86–87, 94, 101, 102, 103, 04–105, 106
Sørensen, Rolf/Jørn Bøhmer Olsen: 46–47, 76, 80, 94–95
Tveit, Torleiv: 15
Væring, O.: 20, 44
Wilse: 18

First published in 1986
by J.W. Cappelens Forlag a·s,
Kirkegt. 15, 0153 Oslo 1, Norway

© J.W. Cappelens Forlag a·s, 1986
Arvid Bryne's text translated by
Joan Henriksen
Layout by Per Syversen
Set by a.s Joh. Nordahls Trykkeri, Oslo
Printed in Centraltrykkeriet Østerås A.S, 1986
ISBN 82-02-10847-0